AWAKEN YOUR CORPORATE ANIMAL

SMART SKILLS TO WIN AT WORK

KARTHIK JAYARAMAN

Chennai • Bangalore

CLEVER FOX PUBLISHING
Chennai, India

Published by CLEVER FOX PUBLISHING 2024
Copyright © Karthik Jayaraman 2024

All Rights Reserved.
ISBN: 978-93-56485-77-8

This book has been published with all reasonable efforts taken to make the material error-free after the consent of the author. No part of this book shall be used, reproduced in any manner whatsoever without written permission from the author, except in the case of brief quotations embodied in critical articles and reviews.

The Author of this book is solely responsible and liable for its content including but not limited to the views, representations, descriptions, statements, information, opinions and references ["Content"]. The Content of this book shall not constitute or be construed or deemed to reflect the opinion or expression of the Publisher or Editor. Neither the Publisher nor Editor endorse or approve the Content of this book or guarantee the reliability, accuracy or completeness of the Content published herein and do not make any representations or warranties of any kind, express or implied, including but not limited to the implied warranties of merchantability, fitness for a particular purpose. The Publisher and Editor shall not be liable whatsoever for any errors, omissions, whether such errors or omissions result from negligence, accident, or any other cause or claims for loss or damages of any kind, including without limitation, indirect or consequential loss or damage arising out of use, inability to use, or about the reliability, accuracy or sufficiency of the information contained in this book.

1. CORPORATE JOB BLUEPRINT

You made it.
You're in the game now.

Now you have a boss, who has a boss of their own.
Work will pile up. You need to get it done.

Be good at what you do. Strike that.
Be great at what you do.

Don't just do what they ask for.
Outperform their wildest assumptions.

But don't be a lone wolf, either.
Be someone your team can rely on.

You'll be working with all sorts of people from all walks of life and circumstances, and that's a good thing.

The company's got bills to pay, salary to provide families and profits are the only way to pay them off.

Your work is going to be scrutinized.
Your quality of output matters and will be in spotlight.

That means your goals will be on the radar.
Your ideas, too. And your deliverables even more so.

Stand up for your work, sell them, make others believe in them if you must, defend their importance, highlight impact, and showcase their potential.

Collaborate as much as you can.
Even if the other team is on another continent
or doesn't exist yet in any shape or form.

Action Box

☐ If you are potentially searching for a job or already joined, discuss with friends or family regarding their perspective or experiences they can share.

☐ Write down any common patterns which could emerge and might prove beneficial in your everyday duties.

☐ Attend networking events, read articles, watch talks by company leaders, browse forums and soak up knowledge and stories.

☐ The more you are in touch with reality, the better chances to survive and excel.

especially not in the Corporate Jungle.

Ready? Let's roll.

~Karthik

*"What we know is a drop,
What we don't know is an ocean."*

**– Isaac Newton
(1642–1727)**

Preface

They're corporate giants, the movers, and shakers of Silicon Valley; the very pinnacle of the tech world.

And guess what?
I didn't just get in; I thrived. I soaked up every lesson navigated every challenge and came out on top, again and again.

Enjoyed it? You bet I did. But it wasn't all smooth sailing. There were lessons learned the hard way.

That's precisely what I'm here to share with you. But before diving in, let's get some things straight.

This book? It's all about the raw and direct talk. No fluff, no filler, just the unvarnished truth.

You're getting the unfiltered revelations as-is that can only come from someone who has lived it.

Each page? Think of it as a rapid-fire coaching session.

We're going to keep it concise, focusing on one actionable revelation at a time.

Because let's face it, you're busy, and you need wisdom that you can apply right now.

My suggestion: Read each chapter at your comfortable pace: Absorb the insight and apply it to your current or potential corporate job situation. Complete the "Action box" recommendations at your convenient time.

You've taken the first step by picking up this book, and for that, you've already earned my respect.

Now, let's get down to business.

There's a lot to cover, and time waits for no one—

And sometimes, they end up feeling overwhelmed or even giving up too soon.

It's like watching a group of well-equipped hikers all set for an expedition, only to find them lost at the first crossroads.

They have the map, the compass, the right shoes – but when the path splits into a dozen trails, the decision paralysis kicks in.

The stress mounts, the pace quickens, and suddenly, those trails seem like unbeatable walls rather than routes to the peak.

This isn't just about workloads or meeting deadlines. It's about navigating the complex, often unwritten rules of the corporate world.

It's about understanding that your career is more than just a job; it's a jungle where the fittest survive, not by brute force, but by wit, resilience, and the ability to adapt.

Now, please allow me to introduce myself.

My name is Karthik and for this reading session, I will be your Guide on this journey if you are willing and open to receiving insights.

Why me? Because I've been in the trenches, building path-breaking products for some of the most amazing High-Tech companies in the industry:

Intel, Microsoft, HP Inc., Palm, and Apple (USA)

What do all these places have in common?

CONTENTS

Preface viii

1. Corporate Job Blueprint..1
2. Own Your Career 5
3. Expect The Expectations 9
4. Your Boss Is An Employee....................................13
5. Stand Out or Move Out..17
6. Bread And Butter 21
7. Hungry For Feedback 25
8. Raging Reactions 29
9. Effective Meetings..33
10. Learning Never Stops...37
11. Embrace Chaos 41
12. S.M.A.R.T Goals 45
13. To Speak Or Not To Speak 49
14. Office Politics...53
15. Friends, Allies, And Rivals....................................57
16. Keep Emotions In Check 61

Contents

17. Choose Your Battles 65
18. Document Everything 69
19. Elevator Pitch 73
20. Burnout Trap 77
21. Credit Theft 81
22. Facing The Unknown 85
23. Own It 89
24. Tough Talks 93
25. The Fellowship 97
26. Job Rabbit 101
27. Body Speak 105
28. Innovation Bank 109
29. The Fine Print 113
30. Wage Warfare 117
31. Signal Ahead 121
32. The Applause 125
33. Storyteller 129
34. The Loop 133
35. Task Stream 137
36. Keepers Of Time 141
37. Product Thinking 145
38. The Guardians 149
39. Tailored Response 153
40. Bias 157
41. Analysis Paralysis 161
42. Managing Money 165

43. Business Travel 169
44. Strong Winds 173
45. Corporate Startup 177
46. Innovation Fortress 181
47. Changing Lanes 185
48. Volunteering Ventures 189
49. AI Worker and Me 193
50. Graceful Exit 197

PREFACE

*D*ear Reader,

Thank you for picking up this book:
"Awaken your Corporate Animal"

The word "Animal" might have caught your eye.
Here, likening to an Animal isn't about ignoring our human essence. Far from it.

It's about embracing the primal qualities that make us exceptional in the corporate ecosystem.

An animal, in its essence, embodies qualities of resilience, adaptability, and an innate drive to thrive. These are not characteristics that diminish our humanity; they amplify it.

So, when I say, "Awaken your corporate animal",
I'm talking about awakening that raw, untamed professional potential inside you.

Every day in my career as a Leader, I interact with so many talented young professionals full of potential but struggle to grow in a corporate office setting.

They've got the skills and the ambition, but they often find it hard to handle the work demands, stress, the pace, the people, and all the rules of corporate life.

DISCLAIMER

The content in "Awaken Your Corporate Animal" is strictly for informational and educational purposes. The author has endeavored to ensure the accuracy and reliability of the chapters provided but does not guarantee their correctness, completeness, or applicability to the reader's individual circumstances.

The views, opinions, and observations expressed are the author's own and do not reflect those of previous or current employers or affiliated organizations.

Therefore, any dependence on the material in this book is strictly at your own risk. In no event will the author be liable for any loss or damage, including, without limitation, indirect or consequential, or any loss or damage arising from loss of data, opportunities, or profits arising out of, or in connection with, the use of this book. The methods and strategies discussed in this book represent the author's personal viewpoints and are provided without warranty of any kind, express or implied. Readers should exercise their own judgment and consult with a professional advisor for their specific situations before undertaking any action or implementing any strategy discussed herein.

The author disclaims any liability for any personal, career, business, or financial decisions made by the reader, emphasizing that the responsibility for any such decisions rests solely with the individual. Any trademarks, service marks, or registered trademarks mentioned in this book are the property of their respective owners.

This disclaimer is intended to be comprehensive and should be reviewed in full. By proceeding with reading this book, you explicitly acknowledge and agree to the terms set forth above.

This book is

DEDICATED

To my parents, Girija and Jayaraman,

To Usha, my wife and better half,

To Harikrishna, our son, a soccer player

To my Mentors who guided me,

To my Guru, who transformed me,

And to the Divine grace of God, above all.

You would need to point out problems when you see them, but also know how to navigate them.
That's why they hired you in the first place.

It'll be fun. It'll be tough.
It'll feel like both at once sometimes.

Friends surround you, but not everyone here gets a gold star for being nice.

Sometimes everything goes right, and sometimes, every episode feels like it drags on forever.

Pressure? Absolutely – it's no quiet corner café.
You are in the express lane during rush hour.

Stress? It depends on how well you deal with it.
Grab a coffee, and we will discuss this later.

Burnout is real, so step back, recognize the signs and act accordingly before it takes over.

In between the craziness, there'll be moments where creativity triumphs, learning happens, and results appear out of nowhere. Treasure those moments because they're your breathers and high fives.

Remember: You're the decision-maker here.

You are the control room operator with a corporate warrior's smile that says, "Bring it on."

Keep your eyes open and stay ready.

Welcome to the corporate world!

* * *

"The only person you are destined to become is the person you decide to be."

– Ralph Waldo Emerson (1803–1882)

2. OWN YOUR CAREER

You own your career.

No one else is going to do it for you.
Not your boss, not your mentor, not your colleagues.

Just YOU!

And no, this isn't some feel-good pep talk.
Pause for a second and let this sink in.

Every day in the office, you may be thinking, I will do this and that, and someone will magically notice your work, recognize you, promote you, and give more of what you wished for.

Here's the absolute, cold, hard truth served straight up. Nobody in the corporate world will hand you success on a silver platter.

You've got to take it. Snatch it yourself.
Own it and make it yours.

First things first. Sit down and think – what in the world do you want? I'm asking beyond "money",

What drives you every day? What makes you tick? What gets you out of bed in the morning and ready for work?
Once you have figured that out, please write it down and slap it on the wall of your room or bathroom mirror.

Map out how you'll get there. Skill up.
Push yourself out of your comfort zone.

Don't just climb the ladder for the sake of climbing.

Action Box

☐ Create a vision book to visually map out your career aspirations and inspirations. Include symbols, words, and pictures that reflect what you desire in your career.

☐ Join a professional group in your field to engage with like-minded individuals, participate and exchange ideas.

☐ Attend industry events and challenge yourself to connect with at least two new people there for sharing experience.

☐ Focus on the feelings and achievements you associate with your career goals.

Craft a unique career that fits your definition of success.
Forge your path with passion and purpose, unbound by conventional constraints.

Troopers of Silicon Valley weren't born at the top.
They hustled. Failed. Learned.
And they then hustled again.

They pushed through the grind, challenges, and obstacles.
Then they figured out their real passion.

That's precisely what we're going to do, too!
Take control, understand where you are located on the grand scale of things, make decisions, and, most importantly, "ACT". EVERY SINGLE DAY.

No excuses, no regrets, no rescheduling, just doing whatever it takes to make our mark.

No hesitations, no what-ifs, no maybes, just stepping into the arena with courage and conviction.

Put in the work, stay focused, and never for a moment doubt your ability to achieve greatness.

Your career isn't something to be won like a lottery ticket.

It's something to be worked on, like art or science. Seek mentorship and collaboration, yet always be the captain of your voyage.

Be patient and persistent, but also believe in yourself.
So, are you motivated enough to own your career? Good!

There is no going back. There's no time like right now.
Let's get started! Are you ready?

* * *

"Duty is that which is expected of us."

– **Ralph Waldo Emerson
(1803–1882)**

3. EXPECT THE EXPECTATIONS

You studied hard. You graduated. You got selected.
You proved your worth. You seized the opportunity.
You negotiated. You signed the dotted line.

Day 1: Welcome letter, company merchandise, salary account configuration, meet and greet session.

Everyone beams with positivity, and you're seen as a valuable addition to the team. Probably you are taken for lunch with your manager.

Day 2: The rubber hits the road.
Look, everyone in the corporate world is either hired to manage expectations or deliver expectations.

Your manager, your colleagues, your cubicle neighbors and even the intern, they all have expectations of you.

Don't know what those expectations are?
Here's an idea: ASK!
"What do you expect from me?"

It's not rocket science; it's communication 101 and preferably get it in writing so they can't say you misunderstood them later.

Managing expectations:
It isn't just about exceeding them. It's about setting clear boundaries, being realistic with what you can deliver, and then delivering more as time permits.

It's a delicate balance between being an experienced realist and a dreamy-eyed cutting-edge innovator.

Action Box

☐ Meet with your Boss, peers, HR team and other experienced employees about your job role's expectations from their perspective. Take notes.

☐ Watch a video or read an article about your role's job duties and responsibilities. The basic expectation could be in the job description when you applied.

☐ Find out a mentor in your role, who is willing to coach or share strategies on how to deal with expectations.

☐ Track your progress towards meeting job expectations and preferably exceeding them

Ambition without attainability is like a rocket without a launchpad – impressive on paper but not going anywhere. We need to get real about the practical stuff, the nuts and bolts that turn our "big ideas" into something achievable.

Corporate overlords expect your goals to follow S.M.A.R.T framework (let's discuss more on this later).

If you manage expectations well, you are already a few steps ahead of your colleague.

In the corporate world being a few steps ahead isn't just about getting there first. It's also about delivery.

It's about setting the pace, raising the bar, and then, when everyone's watching, vaulting over it.

Set those goals (expectations) high but keep them achievable. Then, blow those markers out of the water.

That's how you make waves. That's how you get noticed. And that's how you carve your path from being just another employee to being the one they can't afford to lose.

Have a vision that extends beyond your success.
Success is not measured by the heights we reach but by the depth of our impact on the business.

Vault over the bar, not just with the intent to surpass expectations, but to inspire followers.

Show that the limits we see are often the ones we impose on ourselves. Keep them guessing, keep them impressed,
and above all, keep moving forward.

Let's get to it.

* * *

"He* who cannot obey, cannot command."
– Benjamin Franklin
(1706–1790)

*In the modern age: Replace 'He' with 'Those'.

4. YOUR BOSS IS AN EMPLOYEE

You heard that right.
They're not just another face in the meeting room.
They are one of the gears in the mega-corporate machine.

They might seem quiet, but their role is crucial. They may have the power to promote you or assign additional responsibilities based on your skill set.

But at the end of the day, they clock in and out just like you. This isn't about losing respect; it's about gaining perspective.

Recognizing that they, too, are part of the hustle can bridge the gap between you. Your boss has a world of expectations to deal with – from above (bosses), below (reports), and sideways (teams) in the corporate food chain.

They have quotas, metrics, Key Performance Indicators, centers of excellence, politics, audits and more.

Shift your perspective and level the playing field – because there's no room for me vs them.

Repeat after me – "We're all just trying to make it through."

Understand their goals and pressures, observe their day-to-day challenges ,and see how you can make their life easier.

First approach: align your yearly goals with theirs.
Make it your mission to achieve or fulfill them.

But keep it professional, we're not asking you to fetch coffee for your boss or run their personal errands.

We're asking you to go fetch the results.
Talk solutions, not problems.

Action Box

☐ Schedule one-on-one meetings with your boss at a mutually convenient date and time.1:1 meeting is your time to lead the discussion and should not be used by your boss as a task status update discussion.

☐ Understand their priorities and find out how your work can directly contribute to their success.

☐ Volunteer to lead a small project that aligns with your boss's goals, showcasing your ability to take initiative and deliver results.

☐ Build a good rapport with your Boss and foster mutually beneficial working relation.

Your bosses and managers are not telepathic mind readers.

Present them with ready-made solutions instead of bringing up problems. Be proactive in sharing your thoughts and updates on your projects. You will stand out from the rest.

It's about making their job easier because when they notice that, they'll begin seeing you as a problem solver not a source of headache.

This isn't about doing their job for them or stepping over boundaries – it's about making yourself so invaluable that you set the terms of your career trajectory.

But don't overdo it; being indispensable is one thing, being a doormat is another.

Set boundaries: help your boss level up, but not at the cost of your growth. Maintain a balance that ensures you're developing your skills and advancing your career while supporting your boss's success.

Your boss also gets feedback in the corporate system. From the team, senior leaders, colleagues, and clients. You can provide it, too. It's a two-way street. They are also on a path to learn, correct, and grow.

Remember that everyone's just trying to survive here; your boss included! Helping them succeed means they'll be more likely to return the favor.

It's a no-brainer.
It's not manipulation.
It's mutual progress.

So, are you ready to level up?

* * *

"Be the change that you wish to see in the world."

– Mahatma Gandhi
(1869–1948)

5. STAND OUT OR MOVE OUT

On a random eventful day, possibly after lunchtime, you decide to glance through your job description.

You are in deep thought with a question – "Why am I being asked to perform tasks beyond my job description?"

I frequently receive these thought waves, especially from early career professionals.

See, the job description you applied for is usually the starting point. It's just a general guidance.

It's a map at the beginning of a vast, unexplored territory, hinting at what's expected but not limiting the potential discoveries ahead. It lays the groundwork but leaves room for innovation and personal growth.

Now, you may decide to just stick to what is written in the original job description and not go beyond. Cool. That can work, too. Staying within defined boundaries can provide stability and clarity, ensuring you fulfill what's required without overextending yourself.

But here's the deal:
The middle of a busy road is a risky place to be.
It's where careers go to die a slow, unnoticed death.

You've got two choices: Stand out or Move out.
And since you're not the one to back down, let's talk about leaving your imprint. Making a mark where you are means understanding the nuances of your role and the value you add. Now, standing out isn't about being the loudest in the room or pulling stunts.

It's about being so damn good; they can't ignore you.

Action Box

☐ Conduct a self-audit of your skills and interests, then schedule a meeting with your supervisor to discuss potential projects to contribute beyond your job description.

☐ Arrange a 'Brown bag' or 'Chai Time' presentation to your team on emerging trends or new technology applications.

☐ Organize a weekly discussion group on top issues or industry best practices.

☐ Showcase your initiative and willingness to help solve challenges beyond your scope or domain expertise.

Stand Out or Move Out

It's about solving problems before they become problems. Being proactive not only prevents issues but also positions you as a key problem solver.

It's about being the go-to person for something, anything that adds value. Always look for ways to add value – it could be your knowledge, skills, or simply your attitude.

Skill up. If your job description feels like a straitjacket, it's time to tailor your own suit. Learn something new, even if it's on your time and dime.

Here's another starter: Spot the gaps.
Every team has them, and they're not always about skills. Fill those gaps, be the glue, and suddenly, you're not just a member; you're a cornerstone.

Think two steps ahead of the game. Innovate.
But standing out isn't a solo sport.
It's about lifting others and being the kind of team player who elevates the whole team's game.

But what if you stand out and still find yourself stuck?
Well, that's when you move out.

Not out of defeat but towards a place where your shine isn't just seen; it's sought after. It's about moving to where your unique talents and efforts are not only recognized but also in high demand. The world doesn't need more yes-people.

It needs more problem-solvers and leaders willing to push the envelope and drive us into the future.

Time to choose:
Fade into the background or blaze your own trail.
If you're ready to stand out, then let's get to work.

* * *

"The best investment is in the tools of one's own trade."

**– Benjamin Franklin
(1705–1790)**

6. BREAD AND BUTTER

I understand you got into the big corporate league and are probably a genius at a certain skill or technology.

Coding, product management, marketing, sales; the specific area doesn't really matter.

But if you don't learn the "Real" corporate tools of the trade, you would probably be left behind. These are essential skills—your Bread (Email) and Butter (Calendar)—that are fundamental to navigating the corporate world.

Oh, please! Don't roll your eyes, Einstein! Don't underestimate the importance of mastering these seemingly mundane tools. They play a huge role in daily corporate life and can greatly enhance your efficiency and effectiveness.

Mastery of these tools is what separates rookies from seasoned pros. It's about leveraging them to streamline your work processes and maximize your productivity.

Every email you send reflects you. So, make it sharp, make it clear, and for heaven's sake, make it concise. Clarity and brevity are key to effective communication.

No one has time to scroll through war and peace. Time is a precious commodity, and keeping your communication concise is highly valued. If you don't know how to write a corporate email, get trained on YouTube, Coursera, or LinkedIn.

An email sitting in your inbox for days is a message sitting in limbo. It's not just about communication; it's about Respect.

Think of every email as a handshake – an offer to engage, a nod to connect.

Action Box

☐ Join a course on "Professional Email Communication" and "Time management." In the process, learn about the specific email and calendar applications you use provided by the company IT admin.

☐ Read LinkedIn articles on workplace etiquettes on email and scheduling time.

☐ Observe how your boss or experienced employees write emails or communicate to schedule calendar invitations.

☐ Learn on-the-job and customize your email according to the situation and the audience its addressed to.

Bread And Butter

Calendar is the blueprint of your productivity.

Mastering your calendar is mastering your time.
And guess what?
Time is something that is not manufactured.

Block out time for work, sure,
but also for thinking and strategizing.
Get your calendar under control.

Suddenly, you've got time for everything. And respect other people's time as much as your own.

Double booking, showing up late, canceling last minute? That's amateur hour.

Make "no surprises" your motto.
Keep everyone in the loop with your calendar,
and you'll earn major respect.

And not every ounce of time needs to be squeezed for talking and action. Schedule blanks for zoning out.

Now, don't go overboard, champ.
It's not a task tracker. Look at the bigger picture.

You're going to use these tools to build your empire,
to command respect and to carve out your spot in the corporate universe.

You've got emails to send, schedules to manage, and a career to skyrocket.

Let's get back to work, shall we?

* * *

"Knowing yourself is the beginning of all wisdom."

– Aristotle
(384 BC–322 BC)

7. HUNGRY FOR FEEDBACK

You return home from the office, drop the bag, sit on your couch, and possess a mid-life crisis stare in your eyes.

Why? Did someone give you feedback?
Need not be your manager.

Welcome back to the corporate mind field.

Feedback is your compass, and sometimes,
a hard reality check. Get comfortable with it.

It's just pure, unadulterated insight into where you are doing great, and where you're killing your chances.

But here's where most people screw up:
They take feedback personally.

Snap out of that thought loop. Take a breather.

This isn't about you as a person.
It's about your actions, your work, and your output.

Separate your ego from the equation.

You're here to get better, not to get coddled.
And when you do get that feedback? Act on it.

Be the one who listens, adapts, and evolves.
That's how you grow.
That's how you become indispensable.

See, feedback is less about critique and more about course correction. It's your flight path change to excellence.

Action Box

☐ Initiate a feedback session with a colleague or mentor, asking for specific examples of where you excelled and potential areas for improvement you have overlooked.

☐ Attend a workshop or webinar on receiving and utilizing feedback effectively, focusing on guidance to separate feelings from facts.

☐ Set up a "feedback diary" where you jot down notes and reflections after each feedback session, tracking your emotional responses and the action step you plan to take and observe your growth over time.

☐ Focus on listening and understanding from other's perspective and learning from it.

Look, I get it. No one's perfect.
Think of it this way.

Feedback isn't pointing out flaws.
It highlights opportunities for growth.

And when feedback stings, that's when it's doing its work, etching lessons deep into your career path.

Getting feedback is one thing.
Asking for it is where the real game begins.

That's when you are ready to swim up the river.
It shows initiative, courage, and serious
commitment to your craft.

It puts you in the driver's seat of your career
rather than being a nervous passenger in the middle seat.

So, here's your takeaway:
Be hungry for feedback. Hunt it down. Chew on it.
Digest it. Make it part of your DNA.

Because, in the end, feedback is the fuel that propels you forward, that transforms potential into performance and performance into excellence.

In the corporate world, you're either moving forward or you're falling behind.

And the difference?
It's how you handle feedback.

Stay Strong!

* * *

"The best cure for anger is delay."

– Seneca
(4 BCE–65 CE)

8. RAGING REACTIONS

Listen up. The corporate world?
It's not a petting zoo; it's a jungle.

Your emotional reactions.
They can be your armor or downfall.

So, Bulletproof them. You're going to face criticism.
Not maybe, definitely.

Get this: It's not an attack; it's a gift.
Use it to get better, not bitter.

You'll get frustrated sometimes.
Projects may fail, deals may fall through,
and people may disappoint you.
Let it fuel you, not consume you.

Anger? It's a waste of your energy.

Jealously? Just focus on your lane and your growth. The only comparison that matters is you yesterday vs. you today.

Learn to manage reactions, not let them manage you.
Breathe, think, prioritize, persevere, and conquer.
Rejection is part of the game.

Didn't get that project, promotion, or recognition?
Learn, adapt, try again. It's not the end; it's just a detour.

Success takes time. It's a marathon, not a sprint.
Patience isn't just a virtue; it's a necessity.

Someone or some action "triggered" you.
Reactions raging high? Take a step back.

Action Box

☐ Create a "reaction plan" for common scenarios that trigger strong emotions, detailing steps you will take to channel these feelings constructively.

☐ Practice mindful breathing or meditation few minutes before starting your day or any meeting, to ground yourself.

☐ Emotionally charged discussion or meeting? Take a walk or a snack break.

☐ Observe your reactions when it happens and you will get the knack of the pause.

Reacting in the heat of the moment is like pouring gasoline on a campfire – never ends well.

Bulletproof doesn't mean reactionless.
It means you're the master of your feelings,
not the other way around.

Stress knocking at your door? Let it knock.
You've got things to do and milestones to crush.

Take those reactions, package them,
and when the time's right, unleash them.

Maybe in a presentation, in a pitch,
where they can do some good.

Channel them into something constructive –
exercise, art, journaling.
Make your energy work for you, not against you.

Physical activity is a powerful outlet – run, lift, dance, or find any outdoor activity that helps release reactions and clear your mind.

Practice mindfulness or meditation to gain a deeper understanding of reactions.
End of the day, it's on you.
Own them, manage them, and use them to your advantage.

Remember, it isn't about becoming a robot.
It's about being so mentally tough that whatever the corporate world throws at you, you're ready with your invisible shield.

Game on? Let's dominate.

* * *

*"Luck is what happens
when preparation meets opportunity."*

– Seneca
(4 BCE–65 CE)

9. EFFECTIVE MEETINGS

Ah, Meetings. Perfect for snooze fest or gossip, right?

But really, meetings are not your social hours.
They're the engine room of the corporate world.

First up, just show up on time. Being habitually late?
It's not fashionably cool; it's disrespectfully foolish.

Next up. Come prepared.
Walking into a meeting without doing your homework is like stepping into a gunfight with a water pistol.

Know the agenda, understand the topics,
and please have something to contribute.
Listen more than you can talk.

This isn't the time for your monologue or personal agenda.
But if you're going to add value, by all means, talk.

Take notes. Important stuff gets said, decisions get made, and action points get assigned. If you are proactive, send the Minutes-of-the-Meeting to your team and they may thank you.

Ditch the multitasking.

Reading your inbox while someone's presenting? It's not just rude; it's ineffective. You miss out, and honestly, it shows.

Question time is not your cue to show off trivia skills. If it's relevant, shoot.

Zoom meeting? Yeah, we all love the mute button.

Action Box

☐ Review the meeting agenda, if available, and prepare any necessary documents, questions, or updates you need to share.

☐ Make it a habit to join meetings on time. Being punctual demonstrates professionalism.

☐ Engage actively during the meeting by listening attentively, asking questions, and contributing ideas.

☐ After the meeting, review your notes and follow up on any assigned action items promptly. Set timelines and deliver.

But hit "unmute" often enough to remind folks you're more than just a square on the screen.

Finish up and follow through. The meeting might end, but the real work's just starting.
Be the follow-through master.

Be the one who drives action, not just conversation.
Leave every meeting with clear next steps.
Vagueness is for mystics, not professionals.

And remember, meetings are just the tip of the iceberg.
The bulk of your success lies beneath, in the deep waters of the daily grind.

And here's a hard truth:
Don't make attending meetings your only job.
Not every meeting needs to happen.

Before you schedule another one, ask yourself,
"Could this be an email?"

Respect people's time – yours included.
Keep your contributions sharp and to the point.
If you can say it in five words, don't use fifty.

Time wasted in meetings is time stolen from getting actual work done. Meetings are serious business.

They're where ideas clash, plans form, and decisions are made. Show up, be present, contribute, and execute.

That's how you win in the corporate game.

Enough said. Let's make every meeting count.

* * *

*"He who learns but does not think is lost!
He who thinks but does not learn is in great danger."*

– Confucius
(551–479 BCE)

10. LEARNING NEVER STOPS

Listen, if you think you're finished with learning just because you landed this job, think again.

The fact is the moment you stop learning is the moment you start becoming irrelevant.

And in this fast-paced corporate world?
Obsolescence is the kiss of doom.

Here's the deal: the corporate ladder doesn't care about your certifications or degrees once you're in.

What it cares about is what you bring to the table today, tomorrow, and every day after that.

Are skills getting rusty? Update them.
Don't know the latest in tech or strategy? Learn it.

Your job might not be in a classroom,
but make no mistake, it's still school.

The smartest people know they don't know everything.
So, they listen, they absorb, and they apply.

Got a know-it-all attitude? Drop it.
It's blinding you with its fake perfection.

Knowledge is currency.
Earn it, spend it, save it, invest it.

The classroom's everywhere.
In every project, every task, every "oops" moment.

Action Box

☐ Setup a learning plan with a daily tracker. Reserve at least 30 minutes a day learning anything from technology, finance, sales music or whatever suits your interest.

☐ Read newspapers, magazines, newsletters, Blogs and setup Google alert on key topics.

☐ Participate in a Hackathon or a Project outside your comfort zone.

☐ Embrace the challenge of expanding your skillset and knowledge, allowing your learn-ability muscle to flex and grow.

Remember, the only bad question is the one you never ask.

So, what's the plan?
Be the dinosaur or be the meteor?
Be that person. The one who's always asking,
always curious, always growing.

And here's a hard pill to swallow:
Failure is your best teacher.

You're going to goof up, Jedi! Welcome it.
Every mistake, every miss, is packed with lessons.

Dust off, dissect what happened, and get smarter.

Welcome to the best class, you have ever signed up for.
And pass with flying colors.

Bottom line? Your learning journey is on you.
The company might provide tools or resources, but you've got to be the one to grab them.

Be hungry for knowledge and greedy for improvement.
Rise above the comfort of the familiar.

So, what's it going to be?
Stagnate and get left behind, or evolve and lead the pack?

The choice is yours.

Time to level up.
Learning never stops, and neither should you.

Keep learning!

* * *

"You cannot step into the same river twice."

– Heraclitus
(504 BC–501 BC)

11. EMBRACE CHAOS

So, do you think you have a "steady" job?
Expecting every day to be the same routine.

Let's drill this home:
The corporate world doesn't do stationary.

It's more volatile than the stock market on a busy day. Projects, priorities, and even people – expect them all to change, often when you least expect it.

Stability? It's a myth.
Get comfortable being uncomfortable.

That project you're pouring your soul into might get axed.
Your rockstar teammate might jump ship.

Embrace the chaos. It's in the whirlwind of change that you'll find your greatest opportunities.

Feeling comfy? You're not pushing hard enough.

So, what's your move when the ground shifts beneath you?
Do you freeze, or do you find a new path?

Flexibility isn't just about bending without breaking.
It's about bouncing back, being stronger, and being smarter.

Let go of the illusion of control.

You can't predict every change, but you can control how you respond to it.

Be proactive, not reactive. Anticipate, adapt, and act.

Action Box

☐ Start your day by identifying your top priorities but allow room for unexpected tasks or disruptions.

☐ Utilize organizational tools and systems that can handle the dynamic nature of your work (to-do list apps or planner).

☐ Practice stress-reduction techniques such as mindfulness, meditation, or deep-breathing exercises. Attend in-person courses.

☐ End of day reflect on day's chaos and strategies to manage them in future.

Embrace Chaos

And here's a secret:
The more you get used to change, the less it scares you.

It becomes just another part of the day.

Part of the home furniture, nothing to lose your sleep over.
And when you reach that point, you're golden.

Surfer's mentality: Ride the waves of change with skill and grace, always ready for the next big one.

Newsflash! Mommy and Daddy are not going to hold your hand through this corporate storm.

Hold the hands of change as your mentor, harsh at times, but always driving you toward growth and self-discovery.

Allow yourself to bend without breaking in the harsh winds of change.

It's on you to keep your skills sharp, your mind open, and your spirit unbreakable.

It's about crafting a path that's as unique as you are, one that fits your personal definition of success.
Each gear shift is an invitation to evolve,
pushing you into new realms of possibility.

So, ready to take on the world,
no matter how much it shakes?
Good. Because that's what it takes.

Don't go with the flow, Be the flow.
Time to dive in.
Are you coming?

*   *   *

*"The achievement of one goal
should be the starting point of another."*

– Alexander Graham Bell
(1847–1922)

12. S.M.A.R.T GOALS

Tackling project tasks isn't about throwing something at the wall and seeing what sticks.
It's not going to end well.

You've got to be razor-sharp, laser-focused,
and yes, S.M.A.R.T about it.

But here, "smart" isn't just being clever.
It's Specific, Measurable, Achievable, Relevant,
and Time-bound.

Let's dig in.

Specific?
Define your task. "Improve the app" is vague. "Reduce app load time by 20%" – that's your target.

Measurable?
They are like the checkpoints in a video game. Can't know if you're winning if you don't keep score, right? If you can't measure your progress, you're coding blind. Set those benchmarks.

Achievable?
Ambition's great, but crashing systems isn't. Optimize a component this quarter, not rebuild the entire app. Set goals within your available work capacity.

Relevant?
Align your tasks with project milestones. Working on legacy code when your team's focused on a new feature? Realign. Your code should push the project forward.

Action Box

☐ Clearly articulate what you aim to achieve with each goal. (Specific)

☐ Attach quantifiable metrics to each goal to track your progress. (Measurable)

☐ Realistically assess your resources, limitations, and external factors. (Attainable)

☐ Align goal with your organizations and team's aspirations. (Relevance)

☐ Assign a clear deadline to each goal to encourage timely progress (Time bound)

Time-bound?
Deadlines. They're not just for product launches. Break your goal into sprints (bite-sized pieces). What's done by Friday? Next release? Schedule it.

Pro tip: Put those goals down on paper (not literally!). Write them down on an app or a tool.

There's power in seeing your ambitions spelled out in black and white. It makes them real, tangible, and a heck of a lot harder to ignore or forget.

Each ticked checkbox on your goal list? That's not just progress; it's a high-five to yourself.

Your S.M.A.R.T goals are your waypoints, but your vision is your North Star.

Managers use S.M.A.R.T. goals during performance reviews to set clear expectations for their employees.

Individuals can use the S.M.A.R.T. framework to set goals for personal growth and development.

Keep your eyes on the prize, but don't be afraid to redraw the map to get there. The destination remains the same, even if the journey changes.

Don't just set it and forget it. Regular check-ins on your progress can turn a wish into a reality.

And finally, don't go it alone. Share your goals with a mentor, a colleague, or a friend. Slice through the ambiguity and get it done. Set those goals and crush that project.

Time to get S.M.A.R.T.

* * *

*"Be silent or let thy words
be worth more than silence."*

– Pythagoras
(570 BCE–490 BCE)

13. TO SPEAK OR NOT TO SPEAK

You hear muffled voices, and people shifting in their seats.

You're in one of those team meetings that feels more like a never-ending loop, where everyone's debating left and right, and it all starts to sound like noise after the first 30 minutes.

Then there's you, in the corner, sifting through the chatter, waiting for the right moment.
Finally, you make your point. Time freezes.

The room goes quiet. Heads turn. Energy shifts.

All eyes are on you.
It could turn into a mic-drop moment or
a timely lesson in humility.

Knowing when to open your mouth in the corporate world is an art form. It's not about if you have something to say, it's about when and how you say it.

First step: Read the room.
Is this a brainstorming session where every idea is gold or a cut-throat meeting where words are bullets?

Timing is everything. Speak up when your words add value, not just noise. Make sure your voice is the one that turns heads because it brings clarity, not just volume.

Now, having the guts to speak up, especially with a controversial or unpopular opinion, that's where respect is earned.

But here's a revelation:
It's not just what you say, it's how you say it.

Action Box

☐ Cultivate the habit of taking a brief pause before responding to questions or joining a discussion.

☐ Pay full attention to the speaker and gauge when your input is necessary and meaningful.

☐ In potentially sensitive or contentious situations, ask yourself what your intention is.

☐ Work on understanding the perspectives, feelings, and potential sensitivities of your audience. Empathy and awareness can help you better assess your words.

Confidence matters.

Articulate your points clearly, back them up with facts, and stand your ground.

But please keep it professional.
Let me repeat. Keep it professional.

And here's a hard pill to swallow:
Not every battle is worth fighting, and not every meeting needs your two cents.

Learn to listen as much as you speak.

In the economy of speech, value quality over quantity.

Sometimes, the most insightful person in the room
is the one who says the least.

But don't confuse silence with passivity.
There's power in choosing your moments.

When you do speak, make it count. Make it memorable. Make it so that when you talk, people listen.

Think of the power of silence and speech like the keys of a Piano. The timely combination of the keys and the gaps in between makes memorable music.

So, to speak or not to speak? It's a question of judgment.
It's about striking a balance between making your voice heard and knowing when it's best to hold your tongue.

We've laid the groundwork, now it's go time.
Let's get moving.

* * *

"Bad company ruins good morals"

– Paul The Apostle
(~4 BCE-62 or 64 CE)

14. OFFICE POLITICS

Alright, let's dive into the murky waters of office politics.

You can pretend it doesn't exist,
but that's like ignoring gravity.

It's there, it's real, and if you're not careful,
it'll pull you under.

Without vigilance, it threatens to envelop us.
But here's how you swim without getting dirty.

First rule: Keep your hands clean.

Office politics often resemble the complex and intricate world of Game of Thrones (Big Fan!).

Strategy, betrayal, and the quest for dominance.
But you're not here to play dirty. Stay above the water.

Your integrity? That's your armor.
Don't compromise it for a temporary win.

Know the players and the game. Who holds power? What do they value? Understanding the dynamics at play allows you to navigate them smartly. But remember, you're here to build bridges, not burn them. The walls have ears, and information is currency. The more you know, the better prepared you are to navigate the political landscape without stepping on political landmines.

Gossip is a no-go zone. It's like playing with fire. Steer clear of the rumor mill. Spreading or indulging in gossip only muddies your reputation and sabotages trust.

Action Box

☐ Identify key influencers, decision-makers, and the unspoken rules that govern interactions. This helps you navigate the political landscape more effectively.

☐ Cultivate relationships across different levels and departments within your organization.

☐ Avoid engaging in gossip or alliances that could compromise your values.

☐ Address conflicts constructively, without burning bridges to safeguard your position

Office Politics

Stick to facts and keep your opinions about others to yourself. Operate in the open as much as possible.

The less you hide, the less can be used against you.

Build strong, transparent relationships with colleagues and management. Trust, once established, acts as a buffer against political undercurrents.

Stay focused on your work.
Ultimately, your work speaks louder than any office whisper. Deliver results, and let your success be the noise that drowns out the petty politics.

Your reputation is your most valuable asset.
Guard it by consistently demonstrating integrity, professionalism, and excellence in your work.

Listen, getting caught in the crosshairs happens to the best of us. It's like suddenly finding yourself the main character in a drama you didn't audition for.

Take the high road. Sometimes, the best way to win a game is not to play. By not playing the game, by not retaliating, you're taking control. It disarms the other person because they're expecting a fight, and when it doesn't come, it throws them off.

Remember, navigating office politics doesn't mean you must play the game by other's rules.

You can chart your own course, stay clean,
and still come out on top.

Keep your integrity intact your focus sharp, and get to work. Time to navigate these waters like a pro.

* * *

"All saints have past and All sinners have a future."

– **Anton Chekhov**
(1860–1904)

15. FRIENDS, ALLIES, AND RIVALS

Behold, Oh Loyal Friend of Frodo!
Through treacherous paths and daunting orcs, you stood by him; your loyalty unshaken.

But in the confines of the corporate office,
there are three character types you will encounter:
Friends, Allies, and Rivals.

Figuring out who's who is crucial to your survival and success. You never know who you're dealing with.

Friends at work? It's like finding water in the desert.
If you find one, great, but keep your eyes open.

Listen, work changes people, and pressures can turn friends into rivals in a heartbeat.

Allies? They are your strategic partners.
They're the ones whose goals vibe with yours because you both gain from it. It's all about that win-win. Work together to support each other, but remember, it's conditional. Circumstances change, and so do alliances.

Rivals? They're not the bad guys you see in films. They have their own goals, which might not always match up with yours, but that's okay. Sometimes, a rival can push you to be better so that you can compete harder. Don't make it personal. They're there to set the speed in a race, challenging you to keep up or, better yet, overtake them.

But here's the twist: Roles can change.
One day, you're collaborating, and the next,
you could find yourselves on opposite sides.
Embrace the ebb and flow of office life.

Action Box

☐ Assess and map out your relationships at work (friends, allies and rivals).

☐ Focus on building strong relationships with allies by identifying common goals and how you can support each other.

☐ Treat rivals with respect regardless of personal feelings. Look for areas of mutual benefit where you can work together.

☐ Regarding friendships at work, try to maintain professional boundaries. Avoid any misunderstandings about favoritism.

Friends, Allies, And Rivals

The key? Stay adaptable.

Don't burn bridges unless you absolutely must.
And always, always keep your goals in sight.

Build relationships that help you navigate the complex dynamics of office life.

The workplace is a tapestry of different personalities and sometimes hidden agendas.

Know when to lean on an ally, when to extend an olive branch to a rival, and how to cherish a true friend.

Then, there is the mysterious fourth kind.
Office spies, the unofficial intelligence agents of the workplace can often be a source of concern.

They're the ones always lurking, listening in on conversations, and passing information that isn't theirs to share with your colleagues or your boss.

Be smart about what you share. Just because you hit it off at the team-building event doesn't mean you spill your guts.

And when push comes to shove, protect your own interests.
It's not cynical, it's reality.

Office politics can turn even the best of friends into competitors.

So, are you ready to navigate this battlefield
with your eyes wide open?

Let's get strategic, shall we?
Go out there and play the game!

* * *

"For every minute you remain angry, you give up sixty seconds of peace of mind."

– Ralph Waldo Emerson
(1803–1882)

16. KEEP EMOTIONS IN CHECK

You are probably carrying around a suitcase full of emotional baggage tucked away in the corners of your mind, with all those unspoken words and unresolved emotions.

You have an itch to snap open the suitcase, trying hard to maintain balance in the chaos of existence.

You may be attending your regular office meeting. If you have some disagreement with your boss or colleague or want to express your concern about a topic, all you hear is faint murmurs and the sound of grinding of your teeth.

Then, the moment of expression arrives. And what's your master plan? Unleash the fury in front of everyone and bask in the glory of momentary satisfaction.

All emotions including those unrelated to the meeting escape the well-guarded suitcase.

Brilliant move, right? Wrong.

Let's break it down:
Your boss isn't your therapist, and your colleagues aren't your support group. The workplace isn't a stage for your emotional catharsis. Think unleashing all hell will make you feel better? Maybe. Until you realize you've just torched bridges, credibility, and maybe even your next promotion.

Now, I'm not saying bottle it up. I'm saying be smart.

Angry? Frustrated? Welcome to the club.
It's called "Being an Adult."
Membership requirement:
Handling your emotions like a pro.

Action Box

☐ Try to begin your day with a mindfulness exercise or brief meditation to center yourself.

☐ Identify coping mechanisms that work best for you in managing stress or frustration.

☐ Allow yourself to express your thoughts and feelings openly in a safe environment. Don't just bottle it up, find a way to open it.

☐ Reflect and learn from instances where you managed your emotions well and times you didn't. Train yourself on Emotional Quotient.

Keep Emotions In Check

Suppression? That's so last century.
Understanding emotions is the name of the game.

Take a walk, punch the pillow, scream at the mountain top – whatever floats your boat, as long as it's outside the office.

It's about strategic expression, not emotional explosion. Got it? Good. Nobody wants to be caught in the fallout of your emotional mushroom cloud.

Emotions are like wild horses – if you don't rein them in, they'll run you over. Your emotions are your responsibility. Don't expect others to clean up your mess when you let them run wild.

Bottling up emotions is like shaking a soda bottle and eventually, it's going to explode. So, pop the top and let off some steam responsibly.

When in doubt, talk it out. Silencing your feelings is like pressing the mute button on your own life. Speak up, express yourself, and let your inner voice be heard.

In many companies, there may be outlets like one-on-one meetings, Skip-level meetings, HR helplines, surveys, employee counseling services, or equivalent.

Pause, breathe, and give yourself some perspective:
"Will this matter in the grand scheme of things a month from now?" If not, let it go.

Your career (and your sanity) will thank you for it.
Because at the end of the day, you should focus on unleashing your potential, not your inner Hulk.

Peace out!

* * *

"If a battle cannot be won, do not fight it."

– Sun Tzu
(544 BC–496 BC)

17. CHOOSE YOUR BATTLES

Alright, strap in.
It's time for a little inspiration from military generals.

In the grand chess game of corporate life, not every piece is worth sacrificing your kingdom for.

Translation?
Choose your battles like you choose your food
– wisely and with the end in mind.

Here's the reality check:
You've graduated from the playground.

Not every squabble deserves a battle cry.

Which project management tool should you use?
Pick one and move ahead.

Discussing feature prioritization for a critical project milestone? Now, that's battle-worthy.

Remember, corporate life isn't a sprint.
It's a marathon with hurdles.

Some you jump, some you sidestep.
The trick isn't just in how high you can jump but in knowing which hurdles are worth the leap.

But hey, I get it. You've got principles.
You want to stand up for what you believe in.
A Noble quest, a knight in shining armor.

But let's be real.
Being right isn't the same as being wise.

Action Box

☐ Before engaging in any conflict or confrontation, evaluate the potential impact.

☐ Discuss the matter with a trusted colleague or mentor to gain insights and possibly identify alternative solutions or viewpoints.

☐ Recognize when emotions like frustration or anger are driving your desire to engage in conflict and take time to cool down.

☐ Enhance your negotiation and speaking skills to navigate conflicts effectively.

Sometimes, the wisest thing you can do is bite your tongue, save your energy, and live to fight another day.

So, next time you're itching for a fight, ask yourself:
"Is this worth my time?" or
"Can I channel this energy into something
that moves the needle?"

Remember, in the vast arena of professional life,
battles may be won or lost, but the war persists.

Weigh the costs and benefits before unsheathing your sword and plunging headlong into confrontation.

Standing firm is essential in certain circumstances, especially when the conflict finds its way to your doorstep.

Those are the times when the battle chooses you.

That's when you channel your inner Master Shifu, strategize, and enter the fray with the precision of a surgeon and the impact of a blockbuster finale.

In slow-motion, you walk into that room confidently, your head slowly turns towards your opponents, and they nod a "friendly" gesture; you have already understood their move, every step pre-calculated, backed with data, and you finally settle on that ergonomic office chair like a master tactician ready to face your adversaries with nerves of steel.

Tread the corporate minefield with savvy, poise, and a wink.

Because, let's face it, if you can't find the humor in the office circus, you might be missing the point.

So, lead the way, commander!

* * *

"Those who cannot remember the past are condemned to repeat it."

– George Santayana
(1863–1952)

18. DOCUMENT EVERYTHING

You know those folks who say, "I'll remember that"?
Spoiler alert: They don't.

And neither will you when you're two coffees deep, juggling five tasks, and someone asks you to recall a decision made six months ago on a Tuesday.

Here's the deal:
Your work life is not a '90s sitcom; there are no reruns.

Documenting your contributions, decisions, and yes, even those spicy conflicts are your defense against the
"I never said that" brigade.

Think of documentation as your career's black box.
Those boxes that record everything on an airplane.

When things go south – because let's face it, at some point they will – you've got a record.

It's not about being paranoid. It's about being prepared.

Did you solve a problem? Write it down.

Lead a successful project? Jot it in your victory log.

Did you get into a disagreement over the color of the Post-it notes? Umm, maybe skip that. But if it's substantial? Document it.

Emails are gold.
They're timestamped, easily searchable, and automatically backed up by your company IT Team and solid proof when someone tries to backpedal.

Action Box

☐ Keep a daily log of your tasks, including the specifics of what you accomplished, any decisions made, and communications with team members or clients.

☐ Use email or company-approved messaging platforms that allow for easy tracking and retrieval of conversations.

☐ Create a systematic way of organizing your files, emails, and notes. Use clear and consistent naming conventions for files and folders. Consider IT team recommended cloud storage that allow for secure backup.

But remember, sometimes the IT system gods giveth, and they taketh away. Keep backups of the important stuff.

Hey, a word of caution:
Don't swing the documentation sword to slash and burn.

Use it to illuminate and clarify.
It is not a weapon of destruction but a beacon of clarity.
Wield it with grace and precision, illuminating the path forward rather than casting shadows of doubt.

Unless, of course, you're battling for your rightful credit, then wield it with the finesse of a seasoned knight.

In the grand fabric of your career, documentation is the thread that holds everything together.

It's not just about the destination; it's about the journey, meticulously recorded and celebrated along the way.

It's not about keeping score; it's about keeping track.

In the symphony of your professional journey,
documentation plays the melody, weaving through the highs and lows, the crescendos, and lulls.

So, gear up, future leaders of the boardroom.
Let's turn those key moments into keystrokes.

Let every entry be a testament to your foresight, diligence, and unwavering commitment to thrive in the corporate saga.

Because when history is written –
make sure it's got your name all over it.

* * *

"Plan the sale when you plan the ad."

– Leo Burnett
(1891–1971)

19. ELEVATOR PITCH

Let's talk about the elevator pitch.
You got 30 seconds in an elevator ride with someone important, what would you say to impress them about what you do or your next big idea?

It's your moment to sparkle or flop.

Thinking you can improvise on the spot?
Well, you may be as ready as a snowball in a sauna bath.

The corporate jungle doesn't care for your 'ums' and 'aahs'. You've got the stage, the spotlights on you, and bam! Thirty seconds. That's quicker than your coffee cooling down enough to sip.

Your mission? Make them care, make it stick.

Think of your elevator pitch as a Twitter (X) post for your idea. You wouldn't use a tweet to ramble about your day.

No, you'd make it punchy and impactful.
Apply that to your pitch.

Your idea is the headline, and you're fighting for front-page space in the minds of leadership, not the classifieds.

"But my idea is complex," you say.
Guess what? Nobody's buying complexity.
They're buying solutions, stories, and sparks of genius.

Can you distill your brainchild into a few powerful, captivating cocktail of words?
You better, or you're just serving tap water.

Action Box

☐ Identify the key message or value proposition you want to communicate. What is it about your product that sets it apart?

☐ Practice your pitch out loud. Use a timer to ensure it stays within 30 to 60 seconds.

☐ Share your pitch with friends, family, or mentors and ask for feedback. Use their insights to refine and improve your pitch.

☐ Modify pitch depending on your audience to make it more relevant and engaging.

Now, don't mistake simplicity for superficiality.

This is about depth, about conveying the oceans you navigate in a single drop.

It's art, science, and a bit of magic.

Your pitch should be like a masala chai – perfectly balanced, leaving them warmed, invigorated, and craving for more.

In the world of pitches, less is often more.
Keep it concise and keep it compelling.

Craft it with the listener in mind, making it relatable and memorable. Your elevator pitch is not an oration.
It's a door opener.

It's not about closing the deal on the spot.
It's about piquing interest and sparking curiosity.

Leave them asking for more details,
not looking for the nearest exit.

So, practice. Not in front of your mirror
– your reflection isn't signing any deals.

Test it on real people and gauge reactions
– Refine, Rinse, and Repeat.

Because when the moment comes, that elevator doors close, it's not just about going up.
It's about taking your career with it.

Ready to elevate your game?
Let's get pitching.

* * *

"There is a time for many words, and there is also a time for sleep."

– Homer
(9–8 BCE)

20. BURNOUT TRAP

Greetings, Oh! Noble office knight,
burning the candle at both ends for the Badge of honor?

Aiming for the battle scars and exhaustion trophy, and showing off the medals that collect dust because you're too tired to clean it?

The-Martyr-of-Project pattern.
Let's talk about it. Some of you wear burnout like a medal. "Hey, look at me folks, working myself to the end."

Spoiler alert:
The "end" part isn't as metaphorical as you think.

Hard work? Good.
Non-stop, soul-sucking grind? Not so much.

There's a fine line between dedication and self-destruction.

The corporate world won't tap you on the shoulder and say, "Hey buddy, take a break."

Nope, it'll pat you on the back as you march off the cliff.

And here's the thing: Being busy isn't the same as being productive. Running on a hamster wheel gets you nowhere, except maybe a trip to Burnout city.

Let's not forget the illusion of "If I don't do it, who will?" Remember: The world keeps turning, even if you log off for a few. Shocking, I know!

Don't mix being accountable and taking on everything.

Action Box

☐ Clearly define work hours and follow them. Turn off notifications and avoid checking work emails after certain time.

☐ Learn to prioritize your workload based on urgency and importance. Delegate tasks when possible after discussion with your team.

☐ Short, frequent breaks (walk, stretch) during the workday can improve productivity and creativity while reducing pressure.

☐ Cultivate a trusted network of friends for emotional support and practical advice.

Burnout Trap

Burnout doesn't sneak up; it walks right through the front door you left wide open. Ignoring the signs? That's like ignoring a fire alarm because you're too busy to evacuate.

"I'm fine, just tired." Sniffing with those bloodshot eyes. If that's your mantra, guess what? You're probably not fine. You're a textbook case of burnout in denial.

Your body talks. Headaches, insomnia, that third coffee still not cutting it? That's not normal.
It's your body's SOS signal. Maybe listen?

"Taking a break is for the weak." You still ignore the signs. Congratulations on being the strongest person in a hospital.

Here's a revolutionary thought: Rest. Unplug. Recharge.
It's not laziness; it's called maintenance. Even your smartphone needs recharging, and trust me, you're more complex than a smartphone.

Remember, you're not a machine. Machines don't need sleep, don't enjoy sunsets, and certainly don't cherish moments with loved ones. You do. Or at least, you should.

The Burnout Trap? It's real, and it's lethal. But the exit is always there: balance, self-care, and the radical act of valuing your well-being over your workload.

Take a detour towards a more sustainable path. Discuss with your manager about sharing the workload or taking a break. If the Company can't facilitate these, then you are in the wrong company.

Choose wisely.
Your health, happiness, and sanity depend on it.
It's time to thrive, not just survive.

* * *

"Soldiers generally win battles; generals get credit for them."

– Napoleon Bonaparte
(1769–1821)

21. CREDIT THEFT

Hop on board to the corporate megapolis,
where credit is a currency, and sometimes, it gets stolen.
Right out from under you. Shocked? Don't be. It's almost a corporate rite of passage.

Here's the scoop:
You labor over a project, pour your sweat and tears into it,
and then someone else swoops in and takes the bow.
Feels like a punch in the gut, doesn't it?
Welcome to the club!

The first rule of Credit Club?
Don't lose your cool.
Going nuclear solves exactly nothing.
It might even backfire, branding you as a difficult person.
And trust me, that's a label that sticks.

So, what do you do?
Document your work, your ideas, and your results.
Make it clear and bulletproof that claiming it would be akin to stealing neon signs: glaringly obvious.

Schedule a calm, one-on-one meeting with the person
who took credit for your work, or if necessary,
involve a manager or HR.

Approach the conversation with a focus on seeking recognition for your contributions, not on casting blame.

Speak up but with finesse. It's not about accusing; it's about stating facts. Keep it professional, keep it polite, and most importantly, keep it private.

Next up, Build your brand.

Action Box

☐ Creates tangible records of trail that can support your claims to contributions.

☐ Make it a habit to update your supervisors on your progress and the contributions you're making to projects.

☐ Encourage an environment of open communication and collaboration within your team.

☐ For any issues, take it up directly with the individual in a calm and professional manner, if needed involve HR and manager.

Credit Theft

When you're known for your work,
it's harder for others to claim it as their own.
Be visible.

Share your successes and contributions in meetings, reports,
or casual conversations.

And remember, the best revenge? Outperforming.

Keep delivering knockout punches with your work.

Let your success be so loud that it drowns out any attempts
to dim your shine. Lastly, don't let it turn you cynical.

Yes, credit theft sucks. But it's not the end-all.

Keep doing great work. Keep shining.

The right people will notice. And those who steal credit?
They usually get found out.
Karma's got GPS and a long memory.

In the grand scheme of things, your work speaks for you.
Let it be so powerful, so unique, that even the thought of
stealing it seems like a joke.
They can steal your credit but never your talent.

Edison claimed Tesla's work as his own.
And yet Tesla persisted in his creative endeavors,
prioritizing his groundbreaking ideas over fame.
Today, whose legacy inspired a cutting-edge global brand?

So, chin up, warrior.
You've got battles to win, credits to claim,
and a legacy to build. Onward we go.

* * *

"Our doubts are traitors and make us lose the good we oft might win by fearing to attempt."

– William Shakespeare
(1564–1616)

22. FACING THE UNKNOWN

Suit up because we're diving headfirst into the heart of adventure.

Entering the unknown is like walking into a darkened chamber, not knowing if you're about to discover a chest overflowing with jewels or face an unexpected shadow.

Here's the thing: too many bright, young professionals hit the brakes when they face something new.

"I don't know how" becomes their stop sign.

They wait around for someone to take their hand and lead the way.
Newsflash: That's not how champions are made.

Embrace the unknown. That's your secret mantra.

It's not about having all the answers. it's about finding them, one puzzle piece at a time.

Do you have a project or task that's out of your league or a new skill area to master?
Good. That's your Everest.
Time to climb.

Asking for help isn't the issue,
expecting a full-service guided tour is.
There's a difference.

Be the explorer, not the tourist.
Roll up your sleeves, dive into research,
experiment, fail, learn, and then nail it.

Action Box

☐ Keep a journal of your experiences, including your feelings, challenges faced, and the outcomes of confronting the unknown.

☐ Actively seek out information, advice, and mentorship from individuals with different skills, backgrounds, and experiences.

☐ Identify specific areas where you feel uncertain or lack knowledge. Set clear, achievable learning goals for these areas.

☐ Mindset of learning, correction, and resilience over perfection.

This isn't just about getting the job done.
It's about stretching your limits
and expanding your horizons.

Every unknown you face down is another skill in your arsenal, another story for your victory lap.

Here's a dose of harsh reality:
the corporate world loves problem solvers,
not problem presenters.

Be the first.
Face the unknown with a grin that says, "Try me."

Think of it this way: Every unknown you conquer is another reason for your boss to think twice about who's indispensable. You're not just working; you're showcasing your mettle, your grit. So, what if you stumble?

Every great inventor and every visionary stumbled. They embraced the unknown, wrestled with it, and came out on top. Now, it's your turn.

Remember, the most successful people in history were not those who stayed within the lines. They were the ones who drew new ones, who dared to venture where there was no path and still leave a trail.

Don't wait for someone to hand you the blueprint. Build your own. Yes, it's daunting. Yes, it's challenging.
But it's also thrilling. And when you emerge victorious, you'll realize it was worth it.

Conquer the unknowns. Make them your kingdom.
That's where legends are born.

Ready to take on the next mystery? One unknown at a time.

* * *

"The price of greatness is responsibility."

– Winston Churchill
(1874–1965)

23. OWN IT

Constantly checking your watch, wishing time tick away?
Counting down the minutes until you can log off?
It might seem like a harmless habit.
But wake up. It's a trap, a silent career killer!

Here's the straight shot: Being a clock-watcher?
That's not the gig if you want to leave a lasting legacy.

Every glance at the clock is a moment lost,
a chance for innovation or improvement
that just slipped through your fingers.

Now that you are in the big league,
owning your work isn't just nice; it's necessary.

When you're handed something, be it a project, a task, or whatever; that's your moment.
It's not an inconvenience; it's an opportunity.
To shine, to lead, to say, "This? I've got this,"
and then, to knock it out of the park.

Passing the buck, delaying, not being accountable?
That's old school. That's out.

Today? It's all about grabbing responsibility with both hands and running with it.

Clock watchers, beware. There's a new breed in town.
The owners. The accountable. The movers and shakers who don't just do work; they own it.

And sure, owning it means you might drop the ball sometimes. Guess what? That's okay.

Action Box

☐ Understanding what success looks like for each project or task allows you to take full ownership from the start.

☐ Keep a detailed record of your tasks, decisions, and the reasoning behind them. Helps tracking progress as a reference point for understanding the outcomes.

☐ When mistakes happen, own them openly, learn from them, and share insights with your team to prevent future occurrences.

☐ When projects well, celebrate and recognize.

The corporate world isn't looking for perfection.

It's looking for effort, for ownership, for the guts to say, "My bad, I'll fix it."

It's about becoming indispensable.
The person who doesn't just pass the task but elevates it. The person who, when things go sideways, is part of the solution, not the scenery.

And yes, with great power comes great responsibility.

Owning your work means owning the outcomes,
good or bad. It's about accountability, about being the face behind the success or the hands are fixing the issues.

The narrative of "just doing the job" is outdated, a relic.

The new narrative?
It's about being proactive, about innovation, about thinking not just outside the box but as if there is no box.

Your bosses, your colleagues – they notice.
They see who's just riding the waves and who's making them. Let's not just exist in the corporate world.
Let's live, thrive, and own it.

Your career is not a series of tasks to be completed but a masterpiece in the making.

And you, my friend, are the artist.
Time to own from this moment forward.

Now go work your magic!

* * *

"Fortune favors the bold."

– A Latin proverb

24. TOUGH TALKS

You want to tell your manager to request a change of team, or you want to provide honest feedback to a colleague, or you need to negotiate an extension of the deadline. Recollect situations equally nerve-wracking.

It's like standing at the edge of a high dive, knowing you've got to jump but feel that twist in your stomach.

Those tough, sweat-inducing conversations
are part of the corporate life.

It's like entering a lion's den, but instead of lions,
it's your teammates, your boss, or that intern
who's just not getting it.

Rule number one: Avoidance is not your friend.

Dodging these chats is like ignoring a leaky faucet.
It only gets worse over time.

Face them head-on. Preparation is your armor.

Know what you're going to say before you say it.
This isn't improv comedy; it's real life with real stakes.

Stick to the script, which is the truth.
No embellishing, no sidestepping.
"Here's what happened, and here's how it's affecting things."
Simple, straightforward.

But here's where the magic happens: actually listening.
Not just nodding along while planning your counterattack,
but truly hearing their side. It's enlightening, really.

Action Box

☐ Before engaging in a tough conversation, take time to prepare your key points. Consider the results you hope to achieve and anticipate possible responses.

☐ Practice your delivery to maintain a calm and clear tone, even when the conversation gets challenging.

☐ Maintaining a level of emotional neutrality can help keep the conversation productive and prevent it from escalating.

☐ Have a mindset of win-win outcome.

Focus on the issue at hand,
and keep the low blows out of it.

You're aiming for a solution, not a submission.

This isn't about scoring points.
It's about solving a problem. Together.

"I feel..." – start there to set the tone.

It's personal, yes, but it's also less confrontational.
It's hard to argue with someone's feelings.

And yes, sometimes, despite your best efforts,
it goes off the rails. That's okay. It's not the end.

Take a step back, maybe get some neutral ground
with a mediator and regroup.

This isn't defeat; it's strategy.

Difficult conversations are a test.
They're uncomfortable and challenging
but necessary for growth, for clarity, for progress.

March in there with your facts, your empathy, and your readiness to find a middle ground.

Because what lies beyond these tough talks?
A clearer path forward, a stronger bond, and the respect that comes from facing challenges head-on.

Here's to mastering the art of the tough talk.

Let's do this.

* * *

"Alone we can do so little; together we can do so much."

– Hellen Keller
(1880–1968)

25. THE FELLOWSHIP

You're no lone wolf.

You are part of a pack, a diverse crew thrown together in the quest for greatness.

Picture it like a sports team –
every position is critical, and every player is key.
Collaboration isn't just a nice-to-have; it's survival.

You're not on an island.
You're part of a team, a unit, sometimes chaotic, always dynamic ecosystem.

It's like being part of a band. Sure, you might not get to be the lead singer right away, but every role, from backup vocals to the bass guitar, is crucial.

Learning the ropes?
It's not just about knowing who makes the best coffee or who's the spreadsheet guru.

It's about figuring out how you fit into this puzzle. And trust me, you do fit. Sometimes, it just takes a bit of wiggling.

Giving help is just as crucial as getting it.
See someone struggling? Offer a hand.

Remember, you're building a bridge, not climbing a ladder.
The stronger your team, the stronger your collective output.
It's math, but with people.

And here's where it gets real:
Not every team member is going to be your best buddy.
Shocking, I know.

Action Box

☐ Actively participate in or organize team-building exercises that are both fun and meaningful.

☐ Be a positive force in your team by recognizing and appreciating the efforts and strengths of your colleagues. A simple "thank you" or public acknowledgment can boost morale and foster a supportive and inclusive team culture.

☐ Be open to asking for help when you need it and equally willing to assist others. Offering help strengthens team bonds.

But respect? That's non-negotiable.
You don't have to like everyone,
but you do need to work with them.

Communication is your best friend or your worst enemy.
Misunderstandings are like quicksand for projects.
The clearer you are, the less chance you have of sinking.

Conflict - expect it, confront it, conquer it.
It's not about proving you're right but finding the right solution. Deal with disagreements diplomatically.

One day, you're brainstorming solutions,
the next, you're firefighting unforeseen problems.

Flexibility isn't just nice; it's necessary.

And let's not forget about trust.
It's the foundation of any strong team.

Building it takes time and consistency,
but once it's there, it's the catalyst for unparalleled cooperation and achievement.

A win for your team is a win for you.
It's not about who crossed the finish line first.
It's about crossing it together.

Embrace the mix of minds and talents.
It's the blend that leads to breakthroughs.

And here's the final whistle:
Being on a team teaches you how to win in real life. It's where you get better, face challenges, and become a legend.

"Team, gather up. Your mission awaits."

* * *

"There is no more miserable human being than one in whom nothing is habitual but indecision."

– William James
(1842–1910)

26. JOB RABBIT

You're thinking about job-hopping again, aren't you?
I see that gleam in your eye. <grin>

Yes, tasting the flavors at every corporate or start-up buffet
sounds thrilling. Yum. "Experience," you call it?

Chasing the high of the new job smell,
but let's face it, even new cars lose that scent.

So here we are, staring at your resume,
and it's beginning to resemble a passport filled
with too many stamps, each from a different country.
Each stop is a new adventure, a new "challenge."

But guess what? On paper, you're not seen as the
adventurous hero. You're the flake who can't commit.

Ouch! I know, but someone had to say it.

Employers don't want a teaser trailer.
They want a full-feature film.

"Oh, but I'm broadening my horizons," you say.

Here's the truth: horizons are great, but only if you're going
somewhere, not just hopping on every boat that passes by.

You're collecting jobs like they're limited-edition sneakers.
Spoiler: they're not.

Imagine you're scanning resumes, and there it is,
a career timeline where there is a new company name
every six months to 1 year.

Action Box

☐ Reflect on why you feel the urge to change jobs frequently. Is it dissatisfaction with the role, company culture, a lack of growth opportunities, or external factors?

☐ Define clear, long-term career objectives that go beyond your current position.

☐ Before looking for a new job, explore opportunities within your company that can offer the change or growth you're seeking.

☐ Focus on building strong professional relationships and networks in your company.

What do you think of this resume?
"Dynamic, versatile candidate?" (or)
"I'll leave you at the first sight of a higher paycheck."

"But I'm ambitious," you protest.
Ambition is climbing the ladder, not jumping from one to another, hoping it magically leads to the top.

Real growth? It's about depth, not breadth,
at least after a few years of joining the workforce.

And let's not forget the joy of explaining your job history in every interview. "Why did you leave your last job?"
Oh, to explore new opportunities, you say.
Translation: "I get bored faster than a kid on a family trip."

So, what's the end game here?
The real treasure is commitment.

Staying long enough to make an impression.
But hey, don't just take my word for it.
Go ahead, jump ship again.
Maybe this time will be different.
Maybe this is the job that finally makes you happy,
fulfills you, completes you.

Or maybe, just maybe, you'll start to wonder if the problem isn't the job, but the job-hopper.
Changing jobs like you change TV channels isn't quirky. It's a red flag. You're not collecting experiences;
you're burning bridges. Slow down, champ.
Give each job at least a few years.

Try to focus on what you have and make it work. Because guess what? The grass isn't always greener on the other side. Sometimes it's just AstroTurf.

* * *

"The face is a picture of the mind with the eyes as its interpreter."

– Marcus Tullius Cicero
(106 B.C.E–43 B.C.E)

27. BODY SPEAK

The recent epidemic of the downward gaze.

You've seen them, maybe you are one of them
– the professionals in meetings who act like their shoes are the most interesting conversation partners.

And when it's time to talk?
They look like they're trying to solve a mystery on the floor.

Here's the deal: your body language is screaming,
"I'd rather be anywhere but here."

Crossing your arms – Ah, the classic
"I'm not really open to this."
It's as if you're setting up a physical barrier saying,
"Nope, not interested."

Then there's the leaning back in your chair
during a meeting, the universal sign of,
"I'd rather be watching my favorite episode right now."
It's like you're trying to put as much distance
between you and the real world.

But then, there's the dreaded phone glance.
Mid-conversation, you pull it out just to
"Hey, let me check something really quick."
"I find my phone more interesting than discussion."

You're physically there, but digitally,
you're somewhere else entirely.

Social media addiction?
Sure, let's blame it.

Action Box

☐ Ask your trusted friends or colleagues or even boss on your body language.

☐ Pay attention to your posture, eye contact, gestures, and facial expressions and Identify areas for improvement as the first step toward positive change.

☐ Observe colleagues or leaders whom you consider effective communicators. Take note of their body language.

☐ Practice listening through your body language to better communication at work.

Body Speak

But when your social feed is more fascinating than
real-life humans, you've got a problem.
Attentiveness has left the chat.

Moral of the story?
Your body speaks first before you utter a single word. It can
rally troops or send them running for the hills.

In the workplace, your body language can be the difference
between "leader" and "oh please, not this person again."

Look, I get it.
Social media is a trendy free-spirited haven.
It's like the cool party everyone's invited to,
and real life just can't compete.

Breaking News!
Life isn't lived through a screen.

Lift your head up. Make eye contact.

Show the world you're different than just a profile pic, witty
bio, and more to you than meets the scrolling eye.

Your body language tells your story before you even open
your mouth. What's it going to be?
"I'm barely here" Or "I'm ready to take on the world?"

Uncross those arms, lean in, ditch the digital distractions.
And, for heaven's sake, give a handshake
that doesn't feel like you're passing a dead fish.

Be the master of your nonverbal cues and
watch as the workplace transforms around you.
Because believe it or not, how you say something
often speaks louder than what you say.

* * *

"Not everything that can be counted counts and not everything that counts can be counted"

– Albert Einstein
(1879–1955)

28. INNOVATION BANK

You've got ideas? Cool.
Can you disrupt the status quo? Even cooler.
But here's the million-dollar question:
Can your innovation fill the bank?

Corporate playground doesn't just want your
"Next big thing" unless it's also their
"Next big money-maker."

Got an app that makes emojis dance?
Cute, but can it dance its way into the market
and make investors do the money rain dance?

Think: Is this going to save costs, open new revenue streams,
or at least make the finance team smile for once.

In the glittery world of innovation, it's easy to get
sidetracked by being the next Steve Jobs or Elon Musk.

But slow down, partner.
Those guys didn't just throw darts in the dark.
This isn't about killing creativity.
It's about giving it direction.
Like aiming a water hose at a fire, not at a picnic.

Your brilliance needs to solve real problems, not just look
pretty on a resume or a LinkedIn post.
Think of it this way: Your idea is the seed.
Business value is the sun. No sun, no growth.

You might love your little seed, but if it's not getting any
sunlight, it's just going to be pocket lint.

And nobody's investing in pocket lint.

Action Box

☐ Evaluate your ideas based on the impact they can have on your customers.

☐ Prioritize idea proposals that offer improvements in efficiency, accessibility, sustainability, or user satisfaction.

☐ Develop prototypes of your ideas and test them with real users. Be open to feedback and ready to iterate on your solution.

☐ Seek cross-disciplinary insights which can lead to more holistic innovations.

Let's break it down.
Innovation in the corporate sphere isn't your high school science fair. It's not about what's coolest or most futuristic.

It's about what solves a problem so effectively that people are willing to pay for it, and it translates into long-term revenue streams.
Yes, revenue. That thing that keeps the lights on
and your paycheck signed.

Your idea for a social network for left-handed people? Quirky, yes. Profitable? Hmm, that's a head-scratcher.

Before you sprint down Innovation Lane, do the grunt work.

Who's your market? What's your business model?
And for Dear Lord's sake, how does it make money?

Here's where the rubber meets the road: Practicality.
It's not enough to be new; it needs to be necessary.
"New" catches eyes; "Necessary" open wallets.

So, what's the blueprint for a bankable innovation?
It starts with a problem, a real, gnawing issue that keeps people up at night. Then, you brainstorm, not in a vacuum but with the market in mind. Who feels this pain the most? How have they dealt with it until now? Can you do it better, cheaper, faster? And don't forget about scalability.

Your idea might solve a problem for ten people, but can it scale to solve it for ten thousand? Or ten million? It's not enough to break the internet. You need to break the market.

In the land of innovation, practicality is your passport,
and value is your visa stamp.
Stamp it with authority, and the world is yours to explore.

* * *

"A person without ethics is a wild beast loosed upon this world."

– Albert Camus
(1913–1960)

29. THE FINE PRINT

So, you signed the paperwork, threw a big party, and joined the first day of your job. Congratulations!

But did you realize you automatically agreed to the "Terms and Conditions." Surprised? Did you skip reading it?

Just like that Terms & Conditions popup, you ignore before installing software or the ads you skip on social media.

Yes. That Rule book on the company HR portal which details the Ethics, Rules, Culture, and Guidelines. A concise version must be included in your offer letter, too.

These rules? They're not just there to kill your vibe. Typically, they cover key areas like:

Personal ethics: This is the "how to be a decent human." stuff. It's the line between you and chaos. Overlook this, and it's like you're booking yourself a one-way ticket to employment nowhere.

Professional ethics: This is where you prove you're more than your resume. It's showing up, owning up, and stepping up. Ignore this, and you might as well wear a sign that says, "Professional Liability."

Business ethics: This is where the company's integrity hangs in the balance. Mess this up, and you're not just burning bridges; you're nuking them.

Are rules and ethics for the weak? Think again.

They're what keep the game fair, the fights clean, and the wins legit. You might think dodging them is smart, but here's the real deal: it's a one-way ticket to obscurity.

Action Box

☐ Set aside dedicated time to go through your company's terms and conditions, code of ethics, and relevant policy documents.

☐ Pay attention to sections directly impacting your role and responsibilities, such as data handling practices, confidentiality agreements, and conflict-of-interest policies.

☐ If any part of the terms, conditions, or ethical guidelines is unclear, don't hesitate to ask for clarification from HR or your manager.

The Fine Print

And here's a news flash for you:
The rule book isn't an obstacle; it's your playbook.

Personal ethics keep you grounded, professional ethics keep you respected, and business ethics keep you employed.

And there are other policies and guidelines for reimbursements, travel, time off, performance, and when you can expect that paycheck to hit your bank.

Ignore guardrails? That's not bold; that's a bad strategy. There are other unspoken rules. Enjoy the benefits, but don't lose sight of your responsibilities and the company's trust.

Flexible work hours?
Drop the plan on frequent extended lunch trips.

Remote or Work from Home?
Don't convert it to a movie-watching marathon.

Office supplies: Pens and Post-it notes?
Stop stocking it up in your home.

Company Email?
This is not for your personal use or for a weekly newsletter.

In the cutthroat world of business, being ethical isn't a handicap; it's your hidden superpower.

Read the guidelines of your company and acclimatize.

Wrap your head around them, make them your ally, and watch as you navigate the corporate maze with ease.

It's simple: play smart, play fair, and play to win.
And it all starts with a little thing called ethics.

* * *

"It is not the employer who pays the wages. Employers only handle the money. It is the customer who pays the wages."

– Henry Ford
(1863–1947)

30. WAGE WARFARE

Negotiated with HR, agreed on the compensation details, signed the offer letter, and started your journey.

But the salary comparison saga begins after a few months. Asking colleagues and discussing in anonymous forums, trying to gauge if you're getting short-changed.

Here's the hard truth:
Salivating over someone else's paycheck is like envying someone's vacation photos on social media.
You're only seeing the highlight reel,
not the behind-the-scenes.

Let's get this straight:
Your salary isn't a random lottery number.
It's the result of a bunch of factors: what you bring to the table, how much the market thinks that's worth,
and yes, a bit of company calculus.

It's not personal; it's payroll.
And here you are, plotting your next "I deserve a raise because Robert makes more" speech. Hold your horses.

Do you even know what Robert does? Maybe Robert's negotiating skills were just that good. Or maybe Robert's got skills that you haven't even heard of.

This obsession with what everyone else is earning.
It's like quicksand for your motivation.
Here's an idea: focus on your own game. Up your skills and expand your responsibilities – that's your ticket to a bigger paycheck. Not side-eyeing your deskmate's bank balance.

Asking for a raise isn't about stamping your foot and pointing at numbers. It's a negotiation, not a tantrum.

Action Box

☐ Define your own career objectives that align with your values, interests, and desired lifestyle, rather than focusing on colleagues' salaries as a measure.

☐ Continuously work on improving your skills you are aiming for next and gaining new ones relevant to your field.

☐ Focus on managing your finances wisely.

☐ Regularly remind yourself of your accomplishments, the value you bring to your role and practice gratitude.

Bring to the table what you've done, how you've grown, and where you see your responsibilities going.
It's not about what you want; it's about what you've earned.

Let's not forget the pay bands. They're not just HR's way of being mysterious. They're structured to ensure fairness and consistency. Jumping the band without putting in the work is like skipping to the end of a book.

You miss all the development. And for the love of all that's financially sound, stop making your salary the center of your universe.

Yes, money matters.
But if you're only in it for the paycheck, you're in for a world of dissatisfaction. Passion, growth, and impact – those are the real MVPs that'll drive your career forward.

In the grand scheme of things, your salary reflects your current value to the company, not your personal worth.
So, instead of brewing in salary envy, start building.

Build your skills, build your case, and when the time is right, build your pitch for that raise.

Because here's the thing: Companies reward value.

Be indispensable, be innovative, and most importantly, be patient. The raise will come, and so will the satisfaction of knowing you truly earned it.

Showcase the skills of the next position relentlessly and communicate your achievements regularly.

Do that, and you won't just be asking for a raise
– you'll be proving you deserve one.

* * *

"You may delay but time will not."

– Benjamin Franklin
(1706–1790)

31. SIGNAL AHEAD

Your work is getting delayed or you are unable to attend a meeting, maybe you need more time to prepare for a presentation.

Your response. None. Zilch.
You stay silent.

You assume your co-workers or managers will just know about your situation magically.

Waiting until the zero hour to reveal a delay or absence?
That's not keeping things under wraps.
It's gift-wrapping a disaster.

Listen, surprises are for birthdays, not the workplace.

It's like driving on a highway and encountering a guy on a motorcycle crossing the road from afar and hitting the brakes only at the last second.

You don't swerve at the last second
and expect not to cause a Hollywood car pileup.

You use your indicators. It's about foresight, not hindsight.

Are you worried you'll get grilled if you admit to a delay?
Well, guess what, it's worse if you don't.

It's like waiting until your kitchen is on fire before you tell someone you left the stove on. Not helpful, Sherlock.

And this isn't just about being polite.

It's about respect.

Action Box

☐ Cultivate the habit of looking ahead in your calendar and project timelines. Identify key milestones, deadlines, and meetings early.

☐ Set reminders for yourself to provide updates or heads-ups to relevant stakeholders well in advance.

☐ Communicate regularly ensuring that everyone is on the same page and has sufficient notice to adjust their plans.

☐ Foresee a delay or an issue that could impact timelines and communicate early.

Respect for your team's time, your project's success,
and your own reputation.
You drop a bombshell at the eleventh hour,
and all you'll earn is distrust.

You want to be known as the go-to person, not the run-from person. You might think keeping quiet is the safe play, but it's the silent killer of your credibility.

It's simple. Problems happen, and delays occur.
Leaving issues unaddressed only magnifies them.

It's how you handle them that counts.
Early warnings can be lifesavers.

They show you're in control;
you're proactive, not reactive.

The workplace needs more heroes
and fewer magicians pulling rabbits out of hats.

Say loudly,
"Hey, I've got this, even when I kind of don't."

It shows foresight, accountability,
and that you're playing for the team, not just for yourself.

Next time there's trouble brewing,
Don't zip it. Flip it.

It's time to turn the page from last-minute lament to upfront updates.

Your career will thank you for it.

* * *

"Applause is the spur of noble minds, the end and aim of weak ones."

– Charles Caleb Colton
(1777–1832)

32. THE APPLAUSE

Living for applause in the corporate drama?
You'll be waiting a long time between acts.

Probably, you need a candy, a pat on the back,
a "good job" sticker for every little thing you do?

This isn't a talent show where applause is the prize.

Yes, everyone likes an appreciation or a nod.

It's the corporate world, and here,
the quiet satisfaction of a job well done
needs to be enough.

But if you're only moving your chess pieces for a round
of applause, you're playing the wrong game.

This isn't kindergarten; it's the corporate forest.
The lions aren't clapping for you.
They're assessing your every move.

You may think every task completed deserves a parade.
Here's a reality check:
Doing your job well is exactly what you're supposed to
do. It's like expecting a medal for brushing your teeth.
Well, that's just hygiene.

A little validation doesn't hurt.
It's the fuel that keeps the engine running.

But if you're guzzling it like it's going out of style,
you'll run dry when the going gets tough.

And guess what? It always does.

Action Box

☐ Set personal goals which are meaningful to you independent of external validation.

☐ Dedicate a time each day or any day of the week to go through journaling or a quiet self-care time without distractions.

☐ Seek self-feedback after completion of tasks or projects and ask yourself what went well and what could be improved. Builds self-reliance and confidence.

☐ Surround yourself with like-minded people in the path of self-discovery and growth.

The Applause

Here's a novel idea: self-validation.
That's right, giving yourself a high-five in the mirror.

It's about being your own biggest fan and toughest critic.

Set your bar, reach it, and raise it.

That's how you toughen up, not by collecting
"likes" on your performance report.

Waiting for someone to notice your hard work?
You might as well be watching the paint dry.

Take initiative, and showcase your achievements,
but don't linger for applause.

Move on to the next challenge,
the next opportunity to outdo yourself.

Let your drive come from within, fueled by
a personal quest for excellence,
not by a hunger for external validation.

Turn down the noise of external validation.
Listen to the voice within, pushing you to be better,
to do more, to reach higher.

That's where true growth happens.

That's where you find the strength to stand alone,
knowing you've given your all.

And trust me, when you do, the right kind of recognition
will find its way to you, no applause necessary.

So, ready to be your own cheerleader?
Your squad's waiting.

* * *

"All the world's a stage, and all the men and women merely players."

– William Shakespeare
(1564–1616)

33. STORYTELLER

There you are standing in a dark room
with the projector's light turned on and
the presentation slides are lit partially on your face.

Feels like you're about to reveal the secrets of the universe, doesn't it?

But here's the clicker:
your audience needs enlightenment,
not a black hole of information.

This isn't the time to unleash everything
you know, into the void.

Think of it this way:
You're a chef, not an angry birds game enthusiast.
Serve up that cuisine knowledge meal by meal, not by throwing the whole kitchen at them.

Your goal? To feed, not force-feed.

Dropping abbreviations and jargon like it's hot?
Throwing in complex words like you are a vocabulary contest champion. Slow down, Brainiac.
You're not there to prove you swallowed a dictionary.

Racing through slides like there's a prize at the end?
The only prize is a confused audience.
Pause, breathe, engage. It's not a sprint.
it's a tour through your thoughts.

Translate your genius into something digestible.
It's your chance to make a lasting impression,
It is not a speed-reading contest.

Action Box

☐ Watch videos or TED Talks of your favorite leaders presenting on stage and see how they communicate and deliver the slides.

☐ Rehearse well for your next presentation, understand the audience, their questions and modify your presentation accordingly.

☐ Seek constructive feedback from manager, leads or trusted colleagues on tone, delivery, speech modulation and clarity of message.

☐ Become proficient and train yourself in presentation tools. (Powerpoint or Keynote)

Storyteller

Let your words land. Give them space to breathe.

Make your audience feel they're in good hands, not on a runaway train. And no, it's not a solo performance. Look for nods, puzzled expressions, or drifting attention
—it's your cue to adjust, clarify, or shift gears.

Treat your slides like billboards.
If you need a magnifying glass to read them, you're doing it wrong. Big, bold, and to the point – that's the ticket.
Your audience shouldn't need binoculars.

Remember, a presentation is a story, not a data dump.
Got numbers? Great.
But weave them into a narrative.
Stories stick, and numbers fade.

Be the storyteller, not the number cruncher.
And for the love of clarity, practice.

Rehearse in front of your pet, your plant, or your reflection. Just because it makes sense in your head doesn't mean it will out there. Make sure it flows, not just goes.
End with a bang, not a whimper.
Leave them with something to chew on,
not just "Any questions?" that echoes in a silent room.

Inspire action, provoke thought, or at least, make them glad they didn't skip your coffee session.

In that dimly lit room, with all eyes on you, remember:
You're not just passing on information; you're curating an experience. Simplify, engage, and enlighten.

Ready to light up the room? Let's do this.

* * *

"It does not matter how slowly you go as long as you do not stop."

– Confucius
(551–479 BCE)

34. THE LOOP

Do you feel every day is in repeat mode?
Wake up, grab a coffee, slog through work, crash,
and then start all over again.
It's like being stuck on a merry-go-round, isn't it?

That repetition, that cycle you're so keen to escape.
It's not your enemy. It's actually your undercover
ally in climbing the corporate ladder.

Even something as simple as brushing your teeth
– doesn't feel monumental, but skip it, and things start
falling apart really fast.

Now, you're scratching your head, thinking
– "How is doing the same thing every day going to get me
anywhere?" Good question. I hear you.

Musicians don't become virtuosos overnight.
Athletes don't wake up with Olympic medals.

Okay, back to base. Oscars are not our goal.
The common theme is that these successful professionals
embrace the grind, diving headfirst into repetitiveness, and
transforming it from mundane to mastery.

This is about turning your daily cycle from
a mindless loop into a deliberate practice.

Each day is a new shot at getting a little better, a bit more
efficient, and slightly more impactful.

It's your practice arena, and those seemingly small
repetitions? They're building you up for the big leagues.

Action Box

☐ List down the Daily, Weekly and Monthly achievable goals related to practice and work.

☐ Use mobile apps which track the streak or encourage you not to break the chain.

☐ Reflect on the progress of what you have learned in the day and refine moving forward.

☐ Allocate 30 minutes a day for learning new skill, reading articles or practice a specific task. Consistent dedicated time for learning ensures steady growth.

The Loop

"Sounds like a lot of motivational video fluff,"
you might say. Fair enough.

Do you like to listen to music? I am sure you do.
Have a favorite track that you could loop endlessly?

It's the same thing. It's about those little adjustments to the beat of your daily hustle. Each day, tweak the volume, adjust the bass, and make it sharper and better.

Ever notice how athletes train?
Repetition, routine, cycles.
They're not just working out; they're ingraining excellence into their muscle memory.
Your career needs that same muscle memory.

"So, I just do the same thing over and over? That's it?"
Well, not exactly. It's about setting a cycle of continuous improvement. Wake up, push a little further, refine a little more, and repeat. The cycle isn't a rut unless you stop pushing the boundaries.

"Oh, but routines are so boring."
So does hitting a career plateau.
If the routine feels like a drag, throw in some flair, but whatever you do, don't drop the beat.

The difference between the one who makes it and the one who doesn't? It's those who understand the power of the daily grind and leverage it to their advantage. Consistency is key. Show up, rain or shine.

Talent might open doors, but it's your daily commitment, that'll bulldoze any obstacle in your path.

Don't just ride the bicycle; blaze new trails with it.

* * *

"Division of labor is the cause of wealth."

– Adam Smith
(1723–1790)

35. TASK STREAM

It's 5 pm, and you just nailed that last task.
Ah, the feeling of triumph?

And then, boom, another avalanche of
assignments lands with a thud on your desk.

Feels like an endless buffet of tasks.
But guess what? It's not a curse; it's a blessing.
Confused? Stay with me.

The first thing is to accept the reality of endless work.
And this relentless wave of work means you're needed;
you're in the game.

The real trick?
Learning to juggle without dropping your health
or sanity in the process.

So, the next day, you decide to blaze through your to-do
list like a superhero. Great. But here's the brain teaser:
The faster you clear it, the faster it fills up again.

It's the corporate world's version of "thank you, next."
Don't let that freak you out. It's just the nature of work.

Now, let's talk about the balancing act.

Picture yourself as one of those street performers
spinning plates. Your job, your health, your social life –
they're all wobbling on sticks.
The goal? Keep them all spinning.
Drop one, and it's game over.
Sounds stressful? It doesn't have to be.

Action Box

☐ Make a complete list of work assigned for today, this week and if possible, this month.

☐ Prioritize the list and differentiate between urgent, important, and nice to have tasks. Take the help of a project manager or mentor.

☐ Discuss the priority list and get to a mutual understanding about priorities with your manager. Set clear boundaries. Defer if additional tasks are given without discussion.

☐ Schedule downtime to recharge between meetings, tasks, and work in general.

Efficiency isn't just about speed.
It's about smart moves.
Knowing when to say no, or better yet, when to delegate.

Yeah, that's right. You don't have to be a martyr to your inbox. Share the love and spread the joy of tasks.

Being a work ninja isn't about slashing through tasks at light speed. It's about being smart.

Delegate and negotiate, and for the love of sanity, learn to differentiate between urgent and important.

It's about managing – your tasks, your time, and yes, your downtime. Because you're not a machine.
And even machines need a break.

Work is like a beast that never sleeps.
But guess what? You can take it head-on.

It's about setting boundaries and being the ringmaster, not the tightrope walker.
If you are handed five tasks, don't just dive headfirst as if it's a race for a world record.

Breathe, pause, and consult with your program manager, line manager, or whoever's handing out these tasks.

Directly inquire about the prioritization and due date for these tasks and then plan your execution accordingly.

In this endless buffet, you don't have to clear the tables alone. Share the load, strategize, and enjoy the meal.

After all, it's not about finishing first.
It's about staying in the race.

* * *

"Dost thou love life? Then do not squander time, for that's the stuff life is made of."

– Benjamin Franklin
(1706–1790)

36. KEEPERS OF TIME

As you enter the corridors of the corporate world, it would be that it's not just about technical prowess or specialized skill individuals.

There is a whole array of personnel who live and breathe in the time dimension of the company. The one's handling the processes, timelines, tracks, phases and throwing in buzz words like "Agile" or "Scrum".

They might be named Project Managers, Program Managers, Agile coaches, or Scrum Masters.

Here's the no-frills rundown you need.

First off, understand this: your technical expertise is just one piece of the puzzle. The corporate world runs on processes and methodologies that might seem overkill, but trust me, they're essential. Without them, it's chaos.

Enter Project Management and Agile; the Twin Turbo engines of getting stuff done in today's businesses.

Project management is the art (and science) of steering a project from start to finish, balancing scope, time, and cost.

You'll need to get exposed to timelines, deadlines, and the occasional challenge thrown your way. It's not about doing your job; it's about making sure the entire project crosses the finish line as planned.

Now, Agile is about being fast, flexible, and delivering value in quick iterations. Think of it as sprinting in relay races instead of running a marathon solo.

Action Box

☐ Explore articles, videos on basic concepts of Agile and scrum. Internalized the principles, values, and framework.

☐ Enroll in a course, in-person workshop or webinar for getting formal Agile education.

☐ Discuss with your Program or Project manager on how they manage using Agile and Scrum. Ask questions on latest trends.

☐ Propose a small pilot project with your team and apply the real-life practice of scrum and discover if it's useful or not.

If Agile is the mindset, Scrum is the methodology, a set of practices and roles designed to help teams implement Agile principles. A systematic approach to collaboration.

In Scrum, projects are broken down into sprints, typically lasting two to three weeks. Each sprint is a mini project, complete with its own planning, execution, and review.
An important aspect of Scrum is the stand-up meeting, which teams follow as the "Daily Scrum." It's a quick, focused check-in where each team member answers three questions: What did I accomplish yesterday? What will I tackle today? What obstacles are in my way?

It's about accountability and nipping issues in the bud before they become roadblocks. The roles in a Scrum team are also straightforward. You have the Product Owner, who's like the visionary, knowing what needs to be built and in what order.

Then there's the Scrum Master, part coach, part facilitator, ensuring the team is executing and following Scrum. And finally, the Development Team, the doers, the ones turning ideas into reality.

Scrum thrives on feedback and continuous improvement. At the end of each sprint, there's a sprint review and a sprint retrospective. The review is where the team shows off what they've built, getting feedback to guide future sprints. The retrospective is more about the team looking at what went well and what could be better.

Understanding these basics and project lingo will make you a well-rounded professional who can thrive in a vast process-driven corporate ecosystem.

* * *

"The future belongs to those who believe in the beauty of their dreams."

– Eleanor Roosevelt (1884–1962)

37. PRODUCT THINKING

Believe it or not, there was a time when people were renting or buying DVDs to watch movies.

Heading to the store was like going to a candy shop. Browsing through aisles, spending hours searching for that one movie and occasionally getting zapped with late fees for not returning those rented discs on time.

Enter Netflix.

They didn't just change how we watched movies; they transformed the entertainment landscape forever.

That's the power of product thinking: seeing not just a single solution but a new way of doing things that fundamentally shift behavior on a grand scale.

Netflix's move to streaming was about understanding a deeper need for convenience, variety, and instant gratification in entertainment.

They tapped into our desire not to be tied to TV schedules, to explore a vast library with a few clicks, and yes, to binge-watch without judgment.

So, what does this all mean for you, the aspiring professional ready to make your mark? It means that to really excel, to truly stand out, you need to adopt product thinking in your work, no matter your role.

Creating a product means you're solving a problem on a larger scale. It's the difference between helping a senior carry their groceries home and inventing the shopping cart. One is a good deed, and the other changes the game.

Action Box

☐ Engage with customers or users. Attend a usability research session or a customer feedback discussion in your group.

☐ Participate in design thinking workshops or courses within or outside your company.

☐ Analyze a product you love or use every day and dissect what makes it successful. Explore books or videos on the making of the product or the philosophy behind product.

☐ Start or join a side project in your org or better join a hackathon in nearby cities.

Enter the Product Manager – the visionary, the strategist, the one who navigates between what customers think they want, what they need, and what's technically feasible.

Think of them as the conductor of an orchestra. They might not play every instrument, but they know how to make them all work together to create something beautiful.

But here's the twist: Product thinking isn't just for Product Managers. It's for everyone on the team. Why? Because when you think like a product person, you focus on the big picture, not just your piece of the puzzle.

You're not just coding or selling; you're solving a problem. Building a product is more than just the items on a feature list. It's like planning the best music festival ever. You're not just booking bands. You're creating an experience that attendees will rave about for years.

Understand the problem you're solving. Not just on the surface but deep down. What's the pain point? Who's feeling it? Why does it matter? Can it grow? Can it evolve? And don't forget about the user. What do they need, what do they want, and how can you make their lives better, easier, or a bit more enjoyable?

Finally, iterate, iterate, iterate. The first version of your product won't be perfect. Heck, it might not even be good. But that's okay. Product thinking is about learning, adapting, innovating, and evolving.

Don't just make stuff and tick off those daily task lists. Make products that matter. Think bigger, aim higher. Ready to build?

* * *

"He who has a wise counselor has a great treasure."

– Baltasar Gracián
(1601–1658)

38. THE GUARDIANS

Among the corporate rhythms, buzz, and excitement, have you encountered those mysterious individuals with straight faces who neither waiver nor indulge?

You will see them having deep conversations with the boss or decision-makers where every move needs a subtle nod of consent from them.

The Old Guards.

Not your bosses or managers, but those seasoned pros who've been around the block for a long time. They're like the guardians of the company's lore, wielding influence without the official power to back it up. They might not sign your paycheck but don't underestimate their indirect influence. They're the Gandalfs of the office – minus the magic staff, plus a coffee mug. They have seen winters and survived restructures, mergers, and "new strategic directions" that come every quarter.

They're closer to the bosses because, well, they've had years to prove their worth. They're in that sweet spot between being in charge and being one of the teams, which means they can be your greatest ally or your weirdest nightmare.

So, how do you deal with these office wizards? First off, respect is key, and don't think of them as resistance.
Acknowledge their tenure and the wisdom that comes with it. These folks have a wealth of knowledge.

They know the ins, the outs, the shortcuts, and the bridges. Befriending them is like having the cheat codes for the game.

Action Box

☐ From your perspective, list down your team members and create a RACI matrix.
Responsible, Accountable, Consulted, and Informed.

☐ Highlight the Consulted and Informed group probably would be your old guards.

☐ Observe their interactions and their influence and reach inside the organization.

☐ Arrange for 1:1 meeting or a cafeteria lunch to network with them, understand the history of the org and build mutual respect.

But what if you find yourself on their wrong side? Maybe you're seen as the young upstart, the fresh face threatening to change things up. Or worse, they might see you as encroaching on their territory. Suddenly, every task becomes a minefield, and every email an essay.

Here's the strategy: Understand their motivations, fears, and, most importantly, their goals. Are they aiming for a promotion? Clinging to what they know? Or are you just looking to retire in peace? Knowing this key to navigating their world.

Always keep them in the loop. Seek their advice. When they offer feedback, listen. Really listen. Even if it's about how things were done in the Jurassic era. Sometimes, buried in their "In those days" lecture, you'll find gems of insight that could save your project from disaster.

But what if, despite your genuine efforts, you're still clashing? Not every hill is worth dying on, especially if it means winning the war. Sometimes, letting them have a win on a small issue can build goodwill, and you can cash in later when needed.

Remember, the Old Guards may hold influence, but they're not the only players. Cultivate relationships across the board. The wider your support base, the less any single group can make or break you.

In the end, remember this:
Today's rookie is tomorrow's seasoned Old Guard. Learn from them, the good and the bad.

One day, a newbie will be looking up to you, figuring out how to win you over. Make sure you're the kind of Old Guard you wish you had met on your first day.

* * *

"Measure twice, cut once"

– Giovanni Florio
(1553–1625)

39. TAILORED RESPONSE

Someone meets you in the hallway and asks you a question or a clarification, and then you find yourself at the beginning of time, explaining everything in detail.

What did it look like, who was there, what time was it, and what flavor did they have for breakfast?

Many yawns and blank nods later, they disappear and never come back. People don't have time to listen to all that saga.

People are just looking for insight.
They don't need to know the director's cut of your thoughts – they just want the salad, not the buffet.

I get it. You love showing off your knowledge! And I know how easy it is to turn every question into an hour-long TED talk about something you love. Don't do that.

When someone asks you something,
think twice before responding so that your answer fits perfectly into their question.

Short but sweet answers are an art form.
No more, no less than necessary!

Don't babble about coffee beans when someone asks if there's a cafe nearby. Put yourself in their shoes and give them what they need with simple explanations first.

If even after that they're still lost, then maybe next time try asking them again or maybe ask them first why they want to know instead of explaining so many things in your head.

Action Box

☐ In you next meeting session make it a point to listen actively without judgements or opinions. Sacrifice a few meetings to listening without contributing your genius.

☐ Assess the context, understand your questioner, experience level and background. Cater your response to this individual.

☐ For complex queries, ask clarification and make a mental note and create a reminder to follow-up after further research.

☐ Understand the why before replying.

Tailored Response

Pro tip: Every single time someone asks you anything, pause, reflect, and then respond.

This isn't your usual empty space. Give your brain the much-needed breathing time to process thoughts properly. Otherwise, there's no way you can give the questioner what they need immediately.

Always confirm whether they understood – it's polite and shows respect towards others because very few people care if their message got across clearly or not anymore. Conversation is not a One-way Street.

There are times, you may not know the answer. Just say "I don't know but I can find out." Because pretending doesn't help anybody. Tailor your responses to the audience.

The explanation from the technical team would be completely different from the marketing team, although the questioner and the question are the same.

We often forget: Every single time someone asks you a question, they're also building an image of you.

Are you someone who gives simple answers, or are you sending everyone down rabbit holes?

Next time you are on the spot, remember:
Brevity, clarity, and empathy would go a long way towards great conversations.

Answer cleverly. Respond quickly.

Build an empire out of this corporate jungle!

* * *

"We don't see things as they are, we see them as we are."

– Anaïs Nin
(1903–1977)

40. BIAS

Have you ever seen those people on the beach who wear glasses with yellow frames and blue lenses? They make everything look different when you put them on. In our everyday lives, biases filter into our decisions, interactions, and perceptions of others almost subconsciously.

Here's another way to think about it: When you're tired of listening to songs that don't interest you, you skip through your playlist until your favorites come up without giving any thought to the ones you ignored. That's bias in action.
A bias is a shortcut that helps your brain when it makes decisions more easily.

Maybe there's someone at work who is very loud and outspoken, so you feel like their ideas are always great even though they just talk a lot. Sound familiar?

Your brain tries its hardest to simplify life by relying on patterns it recognizes already. But sometimes, it gets lazy and takes shortcuts through familiar paths, which causes us to miss potentially more rewarding routes entirely.

We won't be discussing whether these shortcuts (biases) are right or wrong, good, or bad—only addressing them comes first. Admit that you're wearing glasses with oddly colored lenses. Then we can work together to take them off.

For example, if you're a Marvel fan and a DC fan shares an idea in a meeting, chances are high that the DC fan's idea will have a lesser chance of acceptance because of your affinity bias of being only around Marvel fans..

Action Box

☐ Talk to your company HR sign up for courses on Bias, Diversity, and Inclusiveness.

☐ When interacting with people or making decisions observe the unconscious bias you are making or someone else is getting into.

☐ Foster an inclusive culture in your team, catch any patterns and resolve them.

☐ Get exposure to communities outside your regular circle and understand their culture, thought process. Socialize with people from diverse backgrounds (art, food, music, books).

One way to counterbalance this affinity (bias) is by surrounding yourself with people outside of what would be considered as "your type."

It could be that agile methodology has solved all your problems before but every time somebody mentions something positive about another methodology (that isn't agile) sparks fly in your head. This could be confirmation bias, by acknowledging this you'll broaden yourself from only one approach being the best to many having value.
When you were first offered a salary quote, that number stuck in your mind, and no matter what offer comes next, that first quote will significantly affect how you perceive any other after that. This is an "Anchor" Bias. Counteract the negative effects by challenging the initial offer.

Leadership shares their opinions in meetings and somehow even though you have data showing a different direction their words stick with you. Maybe because they have more authority at work than you do? This could be an "Authority" Bias. Overcome it by confidently sharing your views that are backed up with data.

One thing that commonly happens during meetings is ideas from male colleagues get immediately nodded to, while very similar suggestions from female colleagues need extra validation or are completely ignored. Sound familiar? That's "Gender" Bias. Unfortunately, it has cousins like "Age" Bias, "Appearance" Bias, "Culture Bias", and "LGBTQ+" Bias. Challenge them all head-on by focusing on contributions purely based on content and impact and not attributes of a person.

Protect yourself with knowledge, ask questions constantly, and remember: the only good bias is the one that's been addressed and remedied.

* * *

"The greatest danger for most of us is not that our aim is too high, and we miss it, but that it is too low, and we reach it."

– **Michelangelo**
(1475–1564)

41. ANALYSIS PARALYSIS

Imagine you're a chef in a busy kitchen.

You've got your ingredients laid out and your recipes at the table. But instead of cooking, you're analyzing every spice, feeling every vegetable, and trying to create the perfect dish. Except your customers aren't getting fed.

In the corporate world, this looks like projects stuck in the research oven, innovations on the back burner, and opportunities cooling off by the second.

It's called Analysis Paralysis – when fear of making an imperfect decision leads to no decision at all.

The belief that one more analysis or one deeper dive will bring up a risk-free solution keeps us from acting.

And as we sit here stalled in time while everyone else is moving forward, unburdened by their need for certainty.

I can hear you thinking: "But I like to research and dive deep into subjects I am passionate about."

I get it, Einstein.
Diving deep and embracing the quest for knowledge is commendable. It's a trait that marks the truly passionate and lifelong learners among us. Nothing wrong with that.

But much like a famous restaurant during rush hour, the corporate world doesn't always afford us the luxury of time for an endless deep dive.

We need swift and decisive action sometimes.

Action Box

☐ Set a decision deadline for your unfinished projects or activities to force into action.

☐ Focus on the 20% of information that will help make 80% of decision. There is nothing called perfect completion.

☐ Chunk your mega initiative into small manageable parts, so decisions could be taken incrementally to break the analysis loop.

☐ Seek external inputs and assistance to measure your project progress and provide much needed clarity in right time.

The key, then, is finding balance.

As you head down into your research, it's important to set deadlines just like a chef uses a kitchen timer.

Timebox the activity in certain sprints and discuss the priority of the activity with your manager.

Remind yourself that these dishes need to be served while still hot and people are waiting to gobble them up.

Encourage a decision-making culture where quick but informed choices are celebrated. Create iterative checkpoint moments where you evaluate how well things are going so far.

Prioritize open communication channels that allow for real-time feedback and adjustments. Make small corrections instead of waiting till the end to see if it came out right

At the end of all this, remember that your work isn't just for you; it's also for your team, clients, and company.

So, keep them in mind as you cook up something nice and timely rather than something perfect but late.

It's about balancing the art of preparation with the art of delivery.

So, keep those stoves firing and the dishes rolling out.

The world's hungry for what you've got to cook up and it's time to serve them right.

* * *

"It is not the man* who has too little, but the man* who craves more, that is poor.

– Seneca
(4 BCE–65 CE)

(*In modern era, replace "man" with "person")

42. MANAGING MONEY

Ka-ching!

And just like that, your salary hits your bank.
And for a brief moment, any complaints leave your mind.

What's next? A night out followed by a shopping spree with your friends? Or maybe you'll buy yourself that brand-new phone or book a last-minute trip to Bali?

The possibilities are endless when you're not looking at the numbers. But here's the thing: While you're having fun, your bank account may barely survive.

Don't get me wrong—being financially stable doesn't mean you have to lock yourself in an office, count coins, and never leave.

It means that one day, you won't wake up and check your bank statement only to realize that someone's cleared all of your money because it was actually you who depleted your wallet with that credit card swipe.

Think of personal finance as a tightrope walk.

You're trying to balance living in the now with saving for the future. Every instant sale you jump into, and every unplanned cruise package deal is another victory for impulse buys but a loss for your future self.

Breaking news:
Waking up to an empty bank account is scarier than any horror movie. "S.O.S." is more terrifying than any thriller movie.

Action Box

☐ Use popular apps or simply write down the budget that accounts for income, savings, expenses, and future goals

☐ Build an emergency fund that could cover 3 to 6 months of your living expenses.

☐ Consult a government registered financial planner or investment advisor to help you grow your money over time (passive income).

☐ Manage your debt wisely and plan to pay off the high interest debt as soon as possible or possibly explore refinancing options.

Taking control of your finances isn't about becoming a hermit who hoards every penny like a rare treasure. You just need to learn when to stop and save instead of acting on impulses.

Budgeting.
It tells you that you can afford one luxury this month but not two or that maybe this month isn't meant for luxuries at all. Maybe start a travel fund. You can take that trip a few months later because you've been setting aside a bit each month.

Investing.
It might sound scary, but it's a good way to grow your money. It's letting your money flex its muscles, even if you're starting small. And yes, there are apps for that, turning your spare change into a growing investment.

Insurance and emergency funds.
They're your safety nets, ensuring that you're not left scrambling when life throws a curveball. It's like putting on your seatbelt – it might not be thrilling, but you'll be glad it's there when you need it.

No one's saying you don't have fun. Life's too short for that. What we're saying is to make a plan. Try to avoid those spur-of-the-moment decisions, ad-hoc adventures, and splurge experiences.

Think of personal finance as the most important project you'll ever manage, where the returns aren't measured in profits but in peace of mind and financial freedom.

It's not about finding creative ways to earn money.
It's about the system where money grows for you.

* * *

"The only way to win is together."

– Saint Augustine
(354–430)

43. BUSINESS TRAVEL

Your boss calls you for a meeting, and instantly, your brain starts flashing through every mishap you've had lately. But once the dust settles, it's revealed that you are being sent to one of the company's other offices on a business trip to another state or even abroad.

Sure, you're being assigned to work, but if you're executing the mission like a SWAT team – touch down, extract, take off – you're missing the plot.

The real deal? It's about diving headfirst into the culture, soaking it up, and learning how to navigate the diverse human landscape.

Culture shock isn't just a buzzword.
It's as real as the jet lag.

When you arrive in a new place, everything from the way people conduct business to how they drink their tea can be completely different. But this is where you take charge. Embrace the differences because understanding and adapting to local customs and etiquette isn't just polite – it's essential for a successful business.

You're not just there to close deals and dash. You're an ambassador of sorts, representing your company, yes, but also bridging the gap between cultures. And this isn't about token gestures, like learning to say "hello" in the local language, though that's a good start.

It's about genuinely understanding what makes the place tick – what is considered respectful, what is frowned upon, and what is celebrated.

Action Box

☐ Before traveling research and familiarize yourself with the cultural norms, language, and etiquette of your destination.

☐ Ensure all meetings, events, and necessary visits are scheduled efficiently to maximize productivity during your trip.

☐ Ensure you have regular communication with home, office, and local contacts.

☐ Create a contingency plan for unexpected situations. Carry documents, cash, medicines, and emergency contact information.

You're not just working with "clients" or "partners;" you're interacting with people who have their own ways of seeing the world. The quicker you grasp that, the smoother your sailing will be.

So, when you land in that new city or country, don't just unpack your business attire; unpack your curiosity.

Dive into the local scene, learn a few phrases of the language, and understand why certain gestures are a no-go and why others can win hearts.

It's this cultural agility that will set you apart back home, turning you into not just a global employee but a global thinker. Embracing differences can transform routine travel into an enriching experience, expanding business horizons and personal growth.

You'll have tales of connections made and cuisines savored. And yes, it can be daunting. You're trying to do a job, after all, not just play tourist.

But think of it this way: the insights you gain, the relationships you build, and the understanding you develop are all part of the package.

They're what can set you apart in a globalized market where cultural intelligence isn't just a nice thing; it's essential.

At the end of the day, business travel isn't a task.

It's an adventure that teaches you not just how to work in a global environment but also how to thrive in it and navigate it with empathy, understanding, and a sense of humor. Because, let's face it, you're going to need it.

* * *

"Doubt is not a pleasant condition, but certainty is absurd."

– Voltaire
(1694–1778)

44. STRONG WINDS

Have you ever wandered down to the seaside near a small and bustling fishing town?

Picture the scene: fishermen or women bustling about in the dim light of dawn, prepping their boats and nets for the day's journey. They venture from the shore into the heart of the ocean, a vast expanse of unknowns. Sometimes, they don't return for days until they've secured their catch.

Just like these fishermen, setting sail into the open sea, we embark on our careers, navigating through calm and turbulent waters, often not knowing what's next.

Here's the unfiltered truth:
Uncertainty isn't just a phase; it's part of the gig. Like weather forecasts in the tropics, expect it to change without much warning.

Job security? As stable as a house made of playing cards. The project you're passionately working on could be axed, tabled, shelved, or de-prioritized. The company you work for might merge, pivot, or tank. The employee working beside you may not come tomorrow.

Uncertainty? It's looming out there in everyone's lives. I am not here to scare you. Just be aware of the surroundings.

Hey now, don't pack up your desk just yet. This isn't doom and gloom; it's the reality check we all need. Because those who thrive aren't the ones who avoid risk; they're the ones who manage it like pros.

Action Box

☐ Summarize your discussions with your manager, colleagues, mentors in a notebook and see if you can identify any patterns.

☐ Read business newspapers, magazines, and social media to identify how your company is doing from the shareholder perspective.

☐ Plan and write down your Plan B and C for any emergency job exit situations.

☐ Keep in touch with your network and community for knowledge and expanding professional relationships.

So, want to be a pro at Risk management?

First, Know your risks. It's not paranoia; it's preparation. Understand the waters you're navigating. Is your industry on a rollercoaster? Is your company in choppy waters? Keep your ear to the ground.

Next up: Build your life raft. That project that feels like it's heading for a nosedive? That creeping sensation that your job might be on the line. Don't ignore them. Face them head-on. Identifying potential pitfalls early gives you the lead time for Plan B.

It's not about being pessimistic; it's about being a realist with optimism. Diversify your skills, like your investment portfolio. Tech guru? Cool, but also sharpen those soft skills. Sales guy? Try to learn data analytics skills.

Next, have a safety net, whether that's a rainy-day bank account, a network in other departments or industries, or a portfolio of projects that showcase your skills. It's the professional equivalent of a life jacket.

Now, when the storm hits, when that project crashes, or when the job slips away, that's when you steer to Plan B. Use every setback as a chance to learn, to pivot, and to adapt. It's not about failing; it's about recalibrating.
Navigating uncertainty isn't a solo journey. Build your circle – mentors, colleagues, an online community.

These are the people who can offer you guidance and insight, maybe even the lifeboat when you need it most.

Will you play it safe on shore, or will you set sail, ready to conquer the rough sea? It's your call.

* * *

"Progress is impossible without change, and those who cannot change their minds cannot change anything."

– George Bernard Shaw
(1856–1950)

45. CORPORATE STARTUP

You may have seen web series or documentaries of the highly successful companies and people of Silicon Valley. Those high-octane stories of overnight success, groundbreaking innovation, and the rise of the underdog. They make it seem like the only path to true innovation is to drop everything, use all your life savings, and emerge as the next big thing in tech.

But here's the jumpstart: that's only one side of the story. Silicon Valley isn't just a place. It's a belief system. It's believing in the impossible enough to make it possible.

It's not an exclusive genius club. It's about being stubborn with your vision but flexible with a plan. It demands you to challenge yourself and push beyond the comfort zone limits you've set.

Think it's all hype? Here's the thing – that mindset is exactly why you have a smartphone in your hand and why you can binge-watch your favorite shows.

It's why you can call a car with a tap or have the world's knowledge in your pocket. They were a bunch of people who were told their ideas were "impractical" but went ahead anyway.

Now, Hang on a second. There's no need for everyone to ditch their secure positions, wave farewell to consistent income, and dive into the rugged rapid-fire world of startups to make a groundbreaking impact.

Even if you want to jump ship and launch a startup, why not try it in your current job and launch your startup skills.

Action Box

☐ Read books and watch movies on the Early Silicon Valley entrepreneurs and their transition to large corporations.

☐ Create a brainstorming meeting with your buddy and list down disruptive ideas from your domain. Then filter the Top five.

☐ Talk to your manager or mentors about the Greenfield projects in your company and ask them if you could participate in meetings.

☐ Attend industry meetups, hackathons, and conferences to broaden your horizon.

Corporate Startup

Say Hello to "The Corporate Startup," the unsung hero of innovation, where risk-taking meets people in a dance. Being part of a "corporate startup" means you're leveraging the might of an established company to fuel innovative projects with a startup's heart.

Imagine having access to the tools, talent, and budget to bring your ideas to life, without the looming fear of failure because let's be real, failure in this setting is just a stepping stone to better solutions. You're in an environment that champions innovation, encourages taking calculated risks, and sees value in learning from mistakes.

So, before you dream of garage startups and venture capital pitches, remember this: innovation isn't confined to the outskirts of Silicon Valley. It's thriving within the walls of corporations willing to think and act like startups. These companies are looking for people like you – yes, you – to challenge the conventional.

There are Greenfield (Pilot) projects. It's you, with an initial team and your ideas, building something from scratch. It's the startup equivalent within a corporation, where you're given the freedom to create new products, services, or processes without the constraints of existing structures.

The Brownfield projects are Innovations with constraints. The challenge of improving, upgrading, and integrating new ideas into existing products for impactful solutions.

So, before you think the only way to make an impact is to write your dramatic resignation letter and venture into the unknown, pause. Look around. The opportunity to innovate, to be part of something bigger, might just be in your current corporate job.

The question now is, are you ready to be that change?

* * *

"Loose lips sink ships."

– United States Office of War Information (OWI)

46. INNOVATION FORTRESS

You just came out of an exciting and buzzing meeting with your team and the leadership.

Hearts racing with excitement about this bleeding edge project. It's big. It's bold.

You are also active on social media and can't wait to post – "Hey wassup, tweeps. We are working on the next big thing in vehicles! Feels like the great move, right?"

Cut to the next sunny morning.

You stroll up to the office as usual with your badge in hand, ready to dive back into the cutting-edge tech. The blinking Red LED beeps – your badge won't work. Security looks at you like an outsider. You're escorted to a room where HR is waiting, not with applause, but with a box for your things. What happened?

Let's rewind. That innocent post? Not so innocent in the world of intellectual property and cybersecurity. Your excitement just breached the fortress of corporate secrets. You invited the world to peek into something that was supposed to be under wraps. Not to mention, your competitors just got a free ticket to your company's thought process.

See, in the digital age, oversharing is more than a social addiction. It's the fastest way to destroy your career and the trust your company placed in you. Cybersecurity isn't just about hackers and firewalls; it's also about knowing when to keep your mouth shut and your posts even tighter.

"But it was just a selfie and a cool caption," you protest.

Action Box

☐ Understand the information you have and have access to in your company. Learn the importance and sensitivity of information.

☐ Complete the corporate training on Information security and watch videos on the dangers of leaking information.

☐ Implement best practices for data protection and sharing sensitive information with stakeholders.

☐ Develop a culture of vigilance. Talk to your manager and colleagues on this topic.

But in the innovation arena, a hint is a peek into the future. It signaled to everyone, that something big was brewing. That's all it takes to expose the next big move.

In the corporate realm, every project, every research, and every innovation is a treasure chest of potential patents. These patents aren't just pieces of paper; they're the shields that defend your company's intellectual property from competitors and copycats alike.

Cybersecurity systems and policies, on the other hand, are the digital shields that protect these innovations from electronic espionage. They guard against the unauthorized sharing of sensitive information that could jeopardize the future of these projects. It's not just about hackers and malware; it's about preventing employees from accidentally giving away the game.

So, when corporations ask you to undergo training on the importance of cybersecurity; it's survival in the digital age. Your post, no matter how simple, becomes a hole in their defenses, a mistake that could cost not just your job but potentially billions in lost revenue and legal battles.

Think about what you're sharing out there. Is it revealing too much? Could it be used against you or your company? Go ahead and post your personal stories with the world. But when it comes to the work that pays your bills and fuels your passions? Keep it under lock and key until the world is ready to see it – on your company's terms. Blend the thrill of innovation with the discipline of discretion. Celebrate your work when your company reveals it at a planned event and shares it in the news or on social media.

Keep your secrets, guard your projects, and someday you will be leading the corporation's next big reveal.

* * *

"Choose a job you love, and you will never have to work a day in your life."

– Confucius
(551–479 BCE)

47. CHANGING LANES

Probably you are an individual contributor or tech lead neck-deep in activities handed down by your manager. As you drag through your to-do list, there's this itch in your head dreaming about that glorious manager title.

Or you are a project manager who wants to become the next director, VP, or senior leadership of the company.

You fantasize about the respect, the authority, the corner office, and the exciting events they are part of.

You are squinting up at them, wondering which one will lead you to the promised land of job satisfaction and a hefty paycheck.

Let's cut through the brain fog.

Are you really considering what stepping into those shoes entails? Or are you just itching for the status bump without pondering the fallout?

Before you leap over the fence because someone else's garden looks flashier, remember, they've got pests too.

Choosing your path isn't about picking the shiniest role; it's about aligning it with what lights you up inside. Let's break it down, shall we?

Tech Leads: You're in the trenches, but you've got the map. You guide the technical direction and make sure the ship doesn't stray off course.

It's less about people management and more about tech mastery and leadership.

Action Box

☐ Perform an honest self-assessment of your strengths and gaps of your career or role (SWOT analysis if possible).

☐ If you have identified a career path or role which you aspire for and then deep dive on the required skills and qualifications.

☐ Research the job description on employment websites with job postings and understand the role expectations.

☐ Develop a detailed transition plan for your new role (short-term, mid-term and long-term).

Architects: You're drawing the blueprints, not laying the bricks. It's big-picture stuff - thinking years ahead, not just about the next sprint. You need a deep understanding of technology to foresee what's coming down the pipeline. If you dream of systems and like complex puzzles, this is it.

Team Managers: It's not just delegation. It's about people. Hiring the right people, retaining them, soothing egos, and sometimes, being the bad cop. You're the layer protecting your team while pushing them forward. It's a role for those who find satisfaction in others' successes and can handle a load of meetings. If you're excited, this is your lane.

Project Managers: The conductors of the tech symphony. You've got an eye on the deadline, a handle on the budget, and a mind that's orchestrating a ton of tasks at once.

Directors: You're the bridge between the ground troops and the generals. You've got a foot in strategy and another in the day-to-day battle.

VPs: The strategists, the visionaries. You're not just part of the game; you're writing the game. It's about spotting opportunities, foreseeing challenges, and setting the course not just for your team but the entire division or company.

All roles in a company play a crucial part in the ecosystem, a unique blend of skills, passions, and perspectives.

So, before you start eyeing the manager's chair or the tech lead's desk, ask yourself: What really gets me fired up?

Choosing your path is a bit like choosing your adventure. So, choose the path that makes you eager to see what the next chapter holds, not just the one that looks best on the cover.

* * *

"The best way to find yourself is to lose yourself in the service of others."

– Mahatma Gandhi
(1869–1948)

48. VOLUNTEERING VENTURES

I think you had enough talk on the daily grind, climbing the ladder, planning your project, chasing a paycheck, disruptive innovation, and changing careers.

Fear not. This chapter is different.

Ever heard of Corporate Social Responsibility (CSR)?

Oh, I hear you, "Not another corporate buzzword."
But stick with me.

This isn't about slapping a green leaf on products or donating to charity once a year for good PR.

Here's the deal: working 9 to 5 and then just binging out on a web series or swiping through social media isn't going to cut it. Not if you want to be part of something bigger.

Corporations aren't just about profits and board meetings. they're about making a dent in the universe. You're young, you've got energy to spare, and you're smarter than you know. Why not channel some of that brainpower and brawn into something that adds up to more than just company profits?

Volunteering, donating, teaching, getting your hands dirty with some fieldwork, and working for a social cause. This isn't about padding your resume or getting a nice photo op. It's about leveraging your skills, and your energy, with corporate support, to do some good.

Maybe you're a wizard at coding, a shark in marketing, or a Master of Design. Now, imagine using those skills for something beyond the corporate.

Action Box

☐ Reflect on causes and issues that resonate deeply in you. Environmental conservation, education, animal welfare, or healthcare.

☐ Research local organizations within your community that aligns with your mission and passion. Reach out to them for helping hand.

☐ Leverage the skills and personal talents to see how you can benefit the burning problems the world or your community faces.

☐ Participate or Donate regularly and build relationships which leads you beyond work.

"But what can I, a normal person possibly contribute? I barely have enough to finish my tasks, let alone relax."
Ah, Glad you brought that up!

Time, or the lack of it, is the classic excuse. It's not about finding time; it's about making it. Swap a couple of TV show hours for something that'll give you more than just entertainment. It'll leave you with a sense of satisfaction and fulfillment.

If your workplace doesn't promote CSR, be the first. Start something. A book drive, coding camp for local kids, a green initiative – wherever your passion takes you.

Propose a project, rally your co-workers, and make it happen. It's not just talk; it's about walking the walk. Showing initiative isn't just good for the soul; it's also good for a career as a side effect. But do it because it feels good, not for the likes or the LinkedIn kudos.

There's something deeply satisfying about lending your expertise to a cause you care about.

This isn't about a guilt trip. It's an opportunity, a way to inject your work life with meaning beyond the monthly paycheck. CSR isn't just corporate lingo.

It's an opportunity, a call to action.

So, contribute, and make it better, not just wealthier.

And who knows? You might just find that in giving back, you get a whole lot more in return without expectation.

* * *

"It is always wise to look ahead, but difficult to look further than you can see."

– Winston Churchill
(1874–1965)

49. AI WORKER AND ME

"Company uses AI automation to replace Humans," "The Great AI takeover," "Humanity at risk due to AI."

These are similar headlines splashed across newspapers and flashing as breaking news on social media. It's like those sci-fi movies when robots are suddenly activated with their eye (cameras) red with fury. They are fed up working for humans and the robot network devises a plan to take over humanity for good. It's enough to make anyone clutch their desk for dear life, wondering when an AI Humanoid will roll in to take over.

These headlines and movie scripts? They love drama. But let's slice through the hysteria with a dose of reality: AI isn't your enemy; it's your co-pilot, your co-employee.

First off, let's bust a myth:
AI is not here to steal your job and send you packing. Sure, it's reshaping the landscape, automating the mundane, and yes, sometimes making certain roles obsolete. But here's the shocker – it's also creating opportunities that require that brilliant human touch, these AI can't replicate.

"Work with AI, not against it," they say. "But what does that even mean? What about the skills I have worked on for years?". AI can crunch data, spot patterns, and even write a decent report (hello managers!), but it can't negotiate a deal with empathy, inspire a team on a Tuesday morning, manage a fire-fighting meeting, or innovate from a blank slate. That's where you come in, armed with creativity, emotional intelligence, and strategic thinking.

Action Box

☐ Make it a point to read long form well researched articles on AI and the industry trends instead of reacting to news headlines.

☐ Focus on enhancing your AI Skills through online courses, webinars, and latest research papers from the academia.

☐ Start a side project for AI collaboration that involve AI components and automation.

☐ Develop complementary skills which AI cannot replace such as creative thinking, emotional intelligence, and communication.

Think of AI as your assistant. It handles the grunt work, leaving you free to tackle the higher-level stuff.

Always wanted to dive deeper into strategy but got bogged down in spreadsheets? AI's got you. Now, you can focus on the "what ifs" and "whys," the areas where human insight shines.

But, "How do I stay relevant in this AI era?" you ask.

The aim isn't to outcompute AI – that's a battle you won't win. It's about enhancing your work, not replacing it. Dive into learning how AI can be your ally in the workplace. Get comfortable with data analytics, familiarize yourself with the latest AI tools, and maybe even try some coding.

The AI wave isn't crashing down; it's lifting all boats. Be the person who not only knows what AI can do but how to leverage it to drive innovation and growth.

Networking isn't just for people anymore. Get to know your AI tools (colleagues). Understand their strengths, weaknesses, and how to collaborate effectively.

Imagine a world where your routine tasks are handled by AI. Suddenly, you've got plenty of time. Time to think, to create, to innovate. Instead of fearing the AI takeover, dream about the AI partnership.

Tackle the big-picture projects, brainstorm new ideas, and lead with a human touch – things AI still can't understand. It's about working smarter, not harder, and certainly not about working yourself out of a job.

Welcome to the era of AI and YOU,
working side by side.

* * *

"All's well that ends well."

– William Shakespeare
 (1564–1616)

50. GRACEFUL EXIT

Oh! You've been planning this moment for a while.

The day you get to send that resignation letter, maybe even dreaming about theatrically throwing your offer letter in your boss's face and probably the keyboard too. Imagining the sheer joy of sailing through your notice period without a care in the world, delaying and stretching time like "Doctor Strange" with his Infinity Stone.

Some of you treat departing like burning bridges, trash-talking your current company, and ghosting employees.

Snap out of it, amigo!
This isn't high school drama. It's your career, and in the corporate world, it's a small, small universe. The corporate sphere is like six degrees of separation (more like two). And your reputation? It's everything.

Today's crash-and-burn exit could easily turn into tomorrow's awkward meetup at an industry conference or even an unexpected encounter with a former boss as a business client.

Here's a thought: Exit gracefully.

It's not about being fake; it's about being smart. You never know when you'll cross paths with these folks again. That manager you bad-mouthed? Turns out they're best friends with your new boss. Awkward!

Instead of burning bridges, how about reinforcing them? A LinkedIn recommendation, a farewell email that doesn't read like an aggressive meme, or even a simple "thank you" can go a long way.

Action Box

☐ Craft a thoughtful resignation letter acknowledging the opportunities and experiences gained in the company.

☐ Create a spreadsheet with transition plan and ensure projects are in order and all pending tasks completed before you leave.

☐ Connect with your colleagues and managers on LinkedIn or Non-work email.

☐ Go out for a lunch with your team and enjoy the moments before your next exciting adventure and endeavor.

That resignation letter? It's not a script for revenge.

This isn't your Oscar moment. No need for dramatics, listing grievances, or shout-outs to those who "always believed in me."

Keep it concise, positive, and professional. Leave the theatrics for the actual actors. A simple "I've learned a lot, and I'm grateful for the opportunities" is your clean goodbye.

And about that notice period – it's not a vacation. It's a testament to your professionalism. Instead of mentally checking out, consider tying up loose ends, documenting your work, and ensuring a smooth transition. It's about leaving a legacy of reliability, not a trail of chaos.

Remember, how you leave a job can be just as important as how you performed in it. Exiting with grace and professionalism isn't just for their benefit; it's for yours.

Because in the end, the world of work is a spinning wheel. Today's entry-level newbie is tomorrow's industry leader.

The impressions you leave now, the professional ties you nurture, they're the seeds for future opportunities.

So, as you plan your exit, aim for grace over grandeur. This isn't about going out with a bang but moving forward with dignity.

Keep it classy, keep it thoughtful, and above all,
keep moving forward.

Time to sign off.
The stage is yours!
(mic drop)

* * *

Made in the USA
Monee, IL
03 May 2026

49438742R00118